Lewis and Clark Revisited

Greg MacGregor

LEWIS AND CLARK REVISITED

A Photographer's Trail

Iris Tillman Hill, Editor / A Lyndhurst Book / published by the Center for Documentary Studies

in association with the University of Washington Press / Seattle and London

Lewis and Clark Revisited: A Photographer's Trail and "The Face of the Country" ©2003 by THE CENTER FOR DOCUMENTARY STUDIES AT DUKE UNIVERSITY
Photographs © 2003 by Greg MacGregor
Maps © Anita Carl and Jim Camp, 1996, 2003

Lewis and Clark excerpts reprinted with permission from *Meriwether Lewis and William Clark, The Journals of the Lewis and Clark Expedition,* 13 volumes. Edited by Gary E. Moulton. Lincoln, Nebraska. The University of Nebraska Press, 1983–2001.

Meriwether Lewis's letters to his mother and to William Clark are taken from *Letters of the Lewis and Clark Expedition, with Related Documents, 1783–1854.* Edited by Donald Jackson. Urbana, Illinois. University of Illinois Press, 1962.

Dayton Duncan's *Out West* is the source of Four Bears's last speech. Lincoln, Nebraska. The University of Nebraska Press, 1987.

The paper for this book meets the guidelines for permanence and durability of the Committee on Production Guidelines for Book Longevity of the Council on Library Resources.

Copyedited by Alexa Dilworth
Designed by Bonnie Campbell

Manufactured in China

Cover photograph: *Missouri River, near Cascade, Montana*
Frontispiece: *Fog on the Lolo Trail, Bitterroot Mountains, Idaho*

Library of Congress Cataloging-in-Publication Data
MacGregor, Greg.
Lewis and Clark revisited : a photographer's trail / Greg MacGregor.
   p. cm.
"A Lyndhurst book published by the Center for Documentary Studies in association with the University of Washington Press."
ISBN 0-295-98342-6 (cloth : alk. paper)—
ISBN 0-295-98343-4 (paper : alk. paper)
1. Lewis and Clark National Historic Trail—Pictorial works. 2. Lewis and Clark Expedition (1804–1806). 3. West (U.S.)—Pictorial works. 4. West (U.S.)—Description and travel. 5. Lewis, Meriwether, 1774–1809—Quotations. 6. Clark, William, 1770–1838—Quotations. I. Duke University, Center for Documentary Studies. II. Title.
F592.7.M24 2003
917.804'2—dc21
2003053110

UNIVERSITY OF WASHINGTON PRESS
1326 Fifth Avenue, Suite 555
Seattle, WA 98101-2604
http://www.washington.edu/uwpress/

Lyndhurst Books, published by the Center for Documentary Studies, are works of creative exploration by writers and photographers who convey new ways of seeing and understanding human experience in all its diversity—books that tell stories, challenge our assumptions, awaken our social conscience, and connect life, learning, and art. These publications have been made possible by the generous support of the Lyndhurst Foundation.

THE CENTER FOR DOCUMENTARY STUDIES
http://cds.aas.duke.edu

FIRST PRINTING
10 09 08 07 06 05 04 03   5 4 3 2 1

FOR JO

contents

THOMAS JEFFERSON HAD a way with words. Whatever the occasion, whatever the subject, he could find just the right phrase to capture the moment or express a compelling idea. Some of those lines—like "life, liberty, and the pursuit of happiness" or "the earth belongs to the living"— have entered our language to become part of the American vocabulary.

When Jefferson drafted exploration instructions for Meriwether Lewis in June 1803, he managed to summarize centuries of speculation and exploration about the fabled Northwest Passage in one sentence. "The object of your mission is to explore the Missouri river, and such principal stream of it, as, by its course and communication with the waters of the Pacific Ocean, may offer the most direct and practicable water communication across the continent, for the purposes of commerce." The expedition's important Native American diplomatic and ethnographic duties were summed up in the order that the explorers record "the names of the nations."

But perhaps the most graceful phrase in the instructions came when Jefferson thought about the western country as it swept out past St. Louis, over the Stony Mountains, and on to the Pacific Ocean. Lewis and Clark were sent out to describe "the face of the country." Jefferson probably did not coin that charming phrase, but it was exactly right considering what a geographically minded president envisioned for his Enlightenment-inspired travelers. As the distinguished historical geographer John L. Allen reminds us, Jefferson was steeped in the geographical literature and lore of his day. The man from Monticello knew that "country" implied more than terrain, more than the sum of mountains and rivers, valleys, and prairies. When Jefferson used the words "face of the country" he meant both the physical character of the West and its promise in the life of the young republic. Looking west from Monticello what Jefferson saw in his mind's eye was the Garden of the World. This was an American Eden blessed with fertile soil, a temperate climate, and abundant supplies of fresh water. The western mountains, all arranged in low, parallel ridges like the Appalachians, would be no barrier to a westering people. And the rivers in the garden—especially the Missouri and the Columbia—were highways of empire linking American farmers to global markets. The Northwest Passage had conveniently moved from the northern reaches of British Canada to lands that might become part of the American nation. It was as if Nature itself had created the West with the American republic in mind.

But it was the promise of the West that most completely captured the president's imagination.

introduction

The Face of the Country

JAMES P. RONDA

The face of the western country could change the face and fate of the nation. Like many of his contemporaries, Jefferson was a passionate believer in the values of republicanism—independence, self-reliance, and self-government. Those virtues grew best in a world of sturdy farmers who worked the land and lived from its produce. More than once Jefferson asserted that if God had a chosen people, they were the farmers. But in a world economy growing ever-more complex and interdependent, the ideal of the small farmer seemed threatened. And in Jefferson's mind the very survival of the American experiment depended on those farmers. For Jefferson the West seemed the answer. Here was a rich country with land enough for generations of stalwart republican farmers. Americans could till the soil, sell their harvests in world markets, and still keep themselves and their nation forever young and free. In a nearly mystical vision of the West, Jefferson conjured up a country that was both a farmers' paradise and a cultural insurance policy against an uncertain future.

The Lewis and Clark Expedition was shaped by Jefferson's prophetic vision of the West. The president's geography of hope directed Lewis and Clark to find a simple West, a face that would smile on American farmers. But looking for simplicity, Lewis and Clark found complexity. Notions about navigable rivers and an easily portaged continental divide dissolved in the fury of white water rapids and a tangle of snow-choked mountains. Expecting to find lands and peoples beyond the hand of change, the explorers encountered countries transformed by generations of human habitation and native people already touched by the Industrial Revolution. Jefferson's garden seemed to exist when Lewis looked out from Fort Mandan and wrote his mother that the northern Plains was "one of the fairest portions of the globe." But just two months later, as the expedition pushed its way up the Missouri in present-day Montana, Clark took his measure of the land and pronounced "This Countrey may with propriety I think be termed the Deserts of America, as I do not Conceive any part can ever be tilled, as it is deficent in water, Timber and too steep to be tilled." And what lay ahead were even more complex and diverse countries—"tremendious mountains," open meadows, rocky river shores, and an ocean Clark declared did not deserve the name "pacific." Lewis and Clark found not one country but many; not one face but many faces.

And there was more. On the day the Corps of Discovery began its journey up the Missouri, Clark wrote that the expedition's "road across the continent" would take it through "a multitude of Indians." Jefferson's "face of the country" was sure to contain many native faces. While the president's words seemed all about landscape and its American future, he and his travelers knew that the West was not an empty place. When Jefferson considered native peoples who called the West home, he was of two minds. Writing in 1803, he branded western Indians as "a cruel and ferocious race." But when a delegation of Missouri River chiefs visited Washington, D.C., three years later, the president claimed that white Americans were "united in one family with our red brethren." Caught between his own admiration for some aspects of Indian culture and a commitment to American imperial expansion, Jefferson could not escape the belief that the faces of the West would eventually be those of white Americans. As he once told Indiana territorial governor William Henry Harrison, native people could either accept American sovereignty and quietly fade away or resist and "we have only to shut our hand to crush them."

What Jefferson fashioned for Lewis and Clark was a fantasy West. No matter what his explorers found, no matter what they reported, that fantasy endured—and endures today. In all sorts of ways, in art, music, literature, film, and advertising, most Americans still hold on to the image of the West as a static place, a kind of museum gallery where nothing ever changes and it is always a golden yes-

terday. But what Lewis and Clark found, and what Greg MacGregor's photographs remind us, is that the West has never been suspended in time and beyond the hand of change. The Lewis and Clark bicentennial marketplace is filled with books that attempt to turn back the clock, to show us the expedition's trail as it might have been in 1804. These photographic explorations have their coffee-table place but they share in and advance the fantasy of the unchanging West.

Two centuries after Lewis and Clark the signs of change are everywhere across the wide Missouri. And they are everywhere in MacGregor's photographs. Rather than artfully screening out dams, powerlines, and amusement parks, his images challenge us to confront our romantic notions about the West. These photographs call out to us, asking us to move beyond nostalgia for an imaginary past or bitterness about a seemingly cluttered present to acknowledge the presence of the daily ordinary—what historian John Brinckerhoff Jackson describes as "the vernacular landscape." A journey on the Lewis and Clark trail today takes us into the heart of that vernacular landscape, countries both ordinary and filled with wonder.

Consider four faces of the country—rivers, plants, animals, and people. Each of these faces interested Jefferson and drew the attention of his explorers. The Lewis and Clark journals are filled with vivid descriptions of surging rivers, exotic plants, remarkable animals, and peoples of all sorts and conditions. Looking at each of these faces as MacGregor found them along the trail today, we take a measure of the changing West.

Jefferson lived on a mountain, but it was rivers that fascinated him. *Notes on the State of Virginia*, his only published book, contains a long section on American rivers. And because for him Virginia was just another name for America, Jefferson included the Mississippi, the Missouri, and phantoms like the Rio Norte and the Salina in his catalogue of waterways. But no river promised more than the Missouri. It was "the principal river," the one that might take adventurers to the eastern edge of the Rockies. Jefferson's rivers defined the country. He not only described them but judged them as well. The yardstick for his judgments was utility, not scenic beauty. The Ohio "is the most beautiful river on earth" but Jefferson quickly let his readers know that the river's real beauty was in its navigability. Rivers existed as highways for empire and commerce. In Nature's grand scheme they were meant to do useful work for human beings. True to Jefferson, MacGregor's photographs show us rivers doing the nation's daily business—carrying cargoes of grain, imported electronics, and casino gamblers.

Jefferson dreamed about western rivers as the Northwest Passage, what poet Walt Whitman later called "the passage to India." Two centuries after Lewis and Clark, the Missouri and the Columbia have become industrial corridors busy generating electricity, turning a profit, and making places for wind surfers. MacGregor's photograph of the Liberia-registered cargo ship *Pacprince* tied up on the Columbia at Longview, Washington, tells the story of global trade and a river at work.

Writing to his friend Charles Willson Peale, Jefferson once described himself as "though an old man, I am but a young gardener." As with rivers, Jefferson measured farms and gardens by their productivity. Monticello's gardens were surely pleasing to the eye but what they grew was for the kitchen and the table. Always eager to find new plants to feed a growing nation, Jefferson instructed his travelers to find and collect the West's "growth and vegetable productions, especially those not of the U.S." In the two and a half years the expedition was in the West Lewis collected and described hundreds of plants. Some 233 samples survive in the Lewis and Clark herbarium. Unlike the simple Garden of the World Jefferson expected, Lewis found everything from the common juniper and the Oregon grape to the field horsetail and the checker lily. In countries of all kinds—in grasslands, mountain meadows, along river banks, and in evergreen forests—Lewis met an abundance of plants in varieties that sparked his imagination. After a brief reconnaissance up the Marias River in present-day north-central Montana, the explorer exclaimed that "it's borders [were] garnished with one continued garden of roses."

Two hundred years later the country's flora is much changed. The ocean of grass that once rolled from Canada to Texas has shriveled to the size of a pond. Railroads, homesteaders, and mechanized agriculture brought monocultures of wheat and corn to the Great Plains. Without sermonizing or offering modern-day laments, MacGregor offers us two emblematic photographs that reveal these changes on the land. One of these shows a field of sunflowers growing on the Lower Brule Reservation in South Dakota. Where once there was prairie grass, now plains farmers plant sunflowers, hoping to press out a profit from their oily seeds. In black and white the sunflowers seem a haunting memory of other days and other plains visions. A second photograph takes us far into the West. On the Columbia, Jefferson's River of the West, grain elevators stand as monuments in the passion to plow and plant with an eye to a global economy. Jefferson's dream of self-reliant farmers working the land by hand has given way to agribusiness, custom-cutter

combines with air-conditioned cabs, and grain for a world market. On Jefferson's river of destiny, the factory has come to the farm.

On a day in late July 1806 Lewis led a small party away from the Great Falls of the Missouri to explore what is now north-central Montana. Surveying the landscape, Lewis wrote that "the whole face of the country as far as the eye can reach looks like a well shaved bowling green, in which immence and numerous herds of buffaloe were seen feeding attended by their scarcely less numerous sheepherds the wolves." What Lewis saw that day is what the expedition witnessed on so many days—a country unimaginably full of life. And more than that, he seemed to sense that the buffalo somehow represented the whole world of the West.

A pair of MacGregor's photographs capture the distance we have traveled from Lewis's day to ours. In one of these images plastic buffalo stand guard alongside a South Dakota highway, bordered by fences and a restaurant-advertising sign. What had once been food now advertises food; what had once been a living, sacred animal now is a mass-produced national icon. Much of the history of the American West can be summed up as an effort to make the West safe for cows, corn, and capital. Cows came in as the buffalo were pushed to near extinction. But nothing is so sure in the West as change. And

MacGregor's lens has caught that perfectly in a photograph of now-abandoned stockyards in Sioux City, Iowa. Those pens and chutes are testimony to changing tastes and markets in a world where today's flavor is tomorrow's throw-away.

Jefferson instructed his explorers to record "the names of the nations," and Clark acknowledged that the West had "a multitude of Indians." The patron and the explorer knew what we often forget; that the West in 1804 was home to thousands of native people. They *were* the "faces of the country." And over the next two and a half years the Corps of Discovery saw Indian faces everywhere. As the Lewis and Clark story unfolded across the country, native people played essential roles in the drama. Food, lodging, route information, guiding, and simple friendship were the native gifts to the strangers. Without those gifts the expedition might well have failed to reach the Pacific.

Lewis and Clark found faces on the land; Mac-Gregor's photographs show us today's western faces along the trail. What the photographs reveal is what Lewis and Clark saw—a human landscape of remarkable diversity. Consider some of MacGregor's images: construction workers building a Missouri River bridge; Sioux boys on a lonely reservation road; Mandan dancers and drummers bringing old rhythms into the present; hikers tramping trails in search of the wide Missouri; holiday-makers splashing in the Lochsa River where the expedition nearly starved; wind surfers on Jefferson's River of the West; and tourists making Fort Clatsop their own end of the trail. Each of these images is a reminder about a fundamental truth in the Lewis and Clark story. The expedition was a human community moving through the lands and lives of other communities. The faces of the country then and now remind us of who we were then, who we are now, and who we might yet become.

Today's Lewis and Clark trail takes travelers though a country of dams, convenience stores, and commercial campgrounds. Hat Rock on the Columbia River is framed by rural mailboxes, a power plant sits atop what was once a Hidatsa village, and high-tension wires lace the sky. But as Greg MacGregor discovered on his journey along the trail, the country also holds memories of an earlier time. The land remembers its past in the shape of hills, the rush of mountain water, and the sweep of the horizon. This explorer's trail remains just that—a way to reveal America in all its complexity, color, and confusion. The many faces of the West still await us, still call out to us. The trail is the way west, the way into the heart of the country.

photographer's note

OTHERS BEFORE ME have crossed the country to photograph in the footsteps of the Corps of Discovery, and in today's America, looking for evidence that a camera can record seems almost a search for fool's gold. Only a single trace of the expedition's passing remains—Clark's signature on Pompey's Pillar in central Montana—and there are very few places where one can stand and be certain that the explorers stood on the same spot—Spirit Mound in South Dakota and Clark's Lookout in Dillon, Montana, are among them. Finding their campsites also proves difficult. Clark drew meticulous maps of the entire route, marking each campsite with a small flag, but the river hasn't cooperated by staying true to its old course. When I went looking for the site of the Iona Volcano, a steaming hill noted by Lewis near Vermillion, South Dakota, I discovered that the entire fifty-foot hill had washed away long ago into flat farmland. I faced another disappointment when I reached the burial site of Sergeant Floyd. His grave had been dug at the top of a bluff; it would now float some seventy feet in the air above the Missouri, far above the heavily eroded banks of the powerful river.

The Corps of Discovery did not have an artist among them, and their journey took place about forty years before photography was invented. A visual record of the landscape as the Corps had seen it wasn't made until 1832 when artist George Catlin followed the Missouri as far as Fort Union, at the mouth of the Yellowstone River. His paintings, however, concentrated on the Indians; the landscape was rarely his primary focus. One year later the German prince Maxmilian steamed up the Missouri on a self-financed journey of exploration with the artist Karl Bodmar on board. Bodmar's excellent watercolors depicted the world traveled by the expedition, including portraits of the Indians and village life as well as superb landscapes in the more scenic areas, such as the White Cliffs and Missouri Breaks region.

It wasn't until the second half of the nineteenth century that survey parties, sponsored by the federal government, documented the West in photographs. These surveys concentrated for the most part on the region well south of Lewis and Clark's route, looking for potential transcontinental railroad routes, exploring unknown rivers such as the Colorado, and hunting for mineral deposits. In searching for twentieth-century photographic documents of Lewis and Clark's trail, I again found only a few, the most notable being *American Odyssey* by Ingvard Henry Eide, published in 1969. Recently, two more books have appeared, attesting to the current popularity of Lewis and Clark, but the photographers have attempted to recreate a landscape undisturbed by the passage of time and the effects of civilization.

In reflecting on the Corps' route and its meaning, I discovered my own point of departure. Wherever a western river flows, it becomes the center for human activities. Power lines, bridges, telephone poles, cities, cattle, recreational facilities, commercial boating, agriculture—all follow the river and grow up along its banks. Hydroelectric dams have created a huge five-hundred-mile-long lake in the Dakotas, and where the Missouri joins the Mississippi at St. Louis the once free-flowing water is channeled in dikes all the way across Missouri, Kansas, and well into Nebraska—for about four hundred miles upstream. These are the changes I accepted and the landscape I chose to record.

Like most people drawn to the story of Lewis and Clark I began with the journals, which were the guidebook and inspiration for my photographs. The journals are immense; in their newest edition they comprise thirteen thick volumes. For my journey I decided to follow the human imprint on the old route, and I searched the journals to find those passages where Lewis and Clark themselves focused on human behavior—their writings about their relationships and exchanges with the men, their meetings with the Indians, and their conversations with themselves during moments of introspection, doubt, and decision-making.

The two captains wrote about different subjects and wrote in different styles. Clark can be counted on to give the daily weather report (fine mornings and disagreeable days march through his entries). He wrote in a plain, matter-of-fact style. Lewis was more lyrical, poetic even, in his descriptions of landscape. However, it was Clark who did most of the writing; Lewis made not a single journal entry for almost a year and a half during the journey.

During the eight years I spent working on this project, one passage from the journals particularly inspired me. Before setting out to photograph another section of the route, I would read again this wonderful passage that Lewis wrote as he left Fort Mandan in the spring of 1805:

Our vessels consisted of six small canoes, and two large pirogues. . . . we were now about to penetrate a country at least two thousand miles in width, on which the foot of civillized man had never trodden; the good or evil it had in store for us was for experiment yet to determine. . . . entertaing as I do, the confident hope of succeeding in a voyage which had formed a dar[l]ing project of mine for the last ten years, I could but esteem this moment of my departure as among the most happy of my life.

editor's note

This book presents a visual journal through contemporary America. Along the way the photographs are accompanied by two different kinds of texts—one taken from the journals of Lewis and Clark, the other written by Greg MacGregor to provide a historical context for the Captains' writings or to tell us about the site he has chosen to photograph.

The writings of Meriwether Lewis and William Clark are one of our country's great historical treasures, made accessible to readers in an extraordinary multivolume set, *The Journals of the Lewis and Clark Expedition,* edited by Gary Moulton. In excerpting the journals for *Lewis and Clark Revisited,* we tried to follow Moulton's edition as accurately as possible, retaining all the original spelling, capitalization, punctuation, spacing, abbreviations, etc. At the same time we were shaping excerpts from the journals, to emphasize a particular story or incident, related in some way to the photographs. Wherever we have deleted words, phrases, or longer passages from the journals, we have indicated those deletions by ellipses. We have retained brackets where Moulton includes them in his edition, and in rare instances we have added a few brackets to mark an insertion by the editor of this book. We have also taken the liberty of not noting ellipses either at the beginning or ending of an excerpt; all the excerpts begin flush left whether they are the beginning of a sentence or not. The Captains used periods eratically, and we have followed their lead by omitting periods within paragraphs and substituting extra spaces for them as Moulton does.

In sequencing the photographs we mostly followed the chronology of the journey of the Corps of Discovery, but the sequence is not always strictly chronological, not always literally attentive to the dates. In selecting and arranging the photographs, in creating a visual narrative, we have on occasion wanted to emphasize the photograph's power in relation to other photographs, and in such cases there is a slight shift in the time frame of the journey. We would ask the readers at such moments in the narrative to study the images as closely as they would the explorers' words so as to see the larger picture.

—IRIS TILLMAN HILL

Lewis and Clark Revisited

Dear Mother,

The day after tomorrow I shall set out for the Western Country . . . my absence will probably be equal to fifteen or eighteen months; the nature of this expedition is by no means dangerous, my rout will be altogether through tribes of Indians who are perfectly friendly to the United States, therefore consider the chances of life as much in my favor on this trip as I should conceive them were I to remain at home for the same length of time . . . For it's fatiegues I feel myself perfectly prepared, nor do I doubt my health and strength of constitution to bear me through it; I go with the most perfect preconviction in my own mind of returning safe and hope therefore that you will not suffer yourself to indulge any anxiety for my safety. . . . You will find thirty dollars inclosed which I wish you to give to Sister Anderson . . . Adieu and believe me your affectionate Son,

Meriwether Lewis

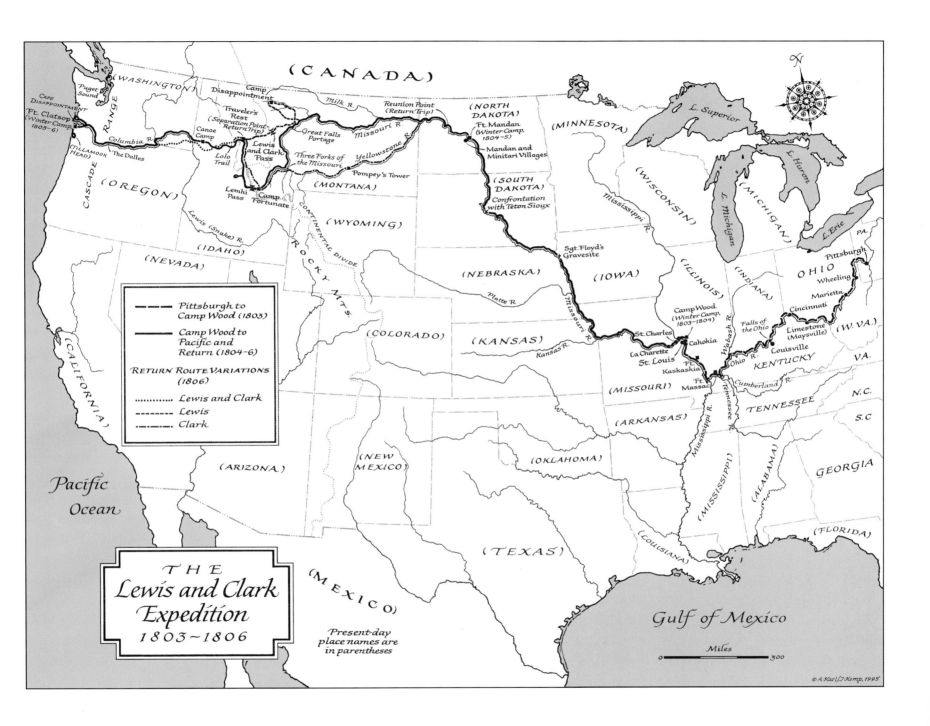

I

I

MAY 21, 1804

<u>Set</u> *out at half passed three oClock under three Cheers
from the gentlemen on the bank and proceeded on to
the head of the Island (which is Situated on the Stbd
Side) 3 miles* —WILLIAM CLARK

Clark and most of the men waited here for Lewis, who
joined them a few days later, and then they were off.
They traveled only three and a half miles that first day,
pulling upstream against the current. Historians dis-
agree about how many men started out on the journey;
their numbers ranged from thirty-eight to forty-two
and included a mix of soldiers, French oarsmen, and
frontiersmen. They traveled in three boats, a large keelboat and two smaller pirogues (open boats with shallow
drafts), which together carried twenty-seven tons. The
Fourth Street Bridge was torn down in 1996.

MAY 23, 1804

We Set out early   ran on a Log and detained one hour, proceeded the Course of Last night 2 Miles to the mouth of a Creek on the Stbd. Side. . . . many people Came to See us, we passed a large <u>cave</u> on the Lbd. Side <Called by the french the <u>tavern</u>> about 120 feet wide 40 feet Deep & 20 feet high   many different immages are Painted on the Rock at this place. the Inds & French pay omage. many nams are wrote on the rock, Stoped about one mile above for Capt Lewis who had assended the Clifts which is . . . at the Said Cave 300 fee high, hanging over the Water, the water excessively Swift to day, we incamped below a Small Isld. in the Meadle of the river, Sent out two hunters, one Killed a Deer
—WILLIAM CLARK

In Lewis and Clark's day the river came up to the cave, which had been used by French traders. In his field notes Clark described here the first of Lewis's several near-death encounters during the journey: "Capt Lewis' assended the hill which has peninsulis projecting in raged points to the river, and was near falling from a Peninsulia. . . . Saved himself by the assistance of his Knife." Today the Missouri Central Railroad tracks cross over the cave's roof. The pile of broken rocks is debris from blasting the cliffs above to create the railroad bed.

3

JUNE 9, 1804

*a fair morning, the River rise a little   we got fast on
a Snag Soon after we Set out which detained us a
Short time   passed the upper Point of the Island
Several Small Chanels running out of the River
below a <Bluff> & Prarie (Called the Prariee of
Arrows) where the river is confined within the width
of <300> yds. . . . opposit the Lower point of the 2d.
Island on the S. S. we had like to have Stove our boat,
in going round a Snag her Stern Struck a log under
Water & She Swung round on the Snag, with her
broad Side to the Current expd. to the Drifting timber, by the active exertions of our party we got her off
in a fiew Mints. without engerey and Crossed to the
Island where we Campd.* —WILLIAM CLARK

On the outbound journey the boats were making about
ten to fourteen miles a day, working against the strong
current from the spring run off. On the return trip,
running downstream and encouraged by the nearness
of their journey's end, Clark noted that they had
traveled seventy-two miles in a single day, as the men,
"plied their ors." The banks of the Missouri near the
state capitol have been reinforced with concrete debris
to form a levee against floods. Towns and cities sit atop
these bluffs or on nearby high land, but here the river's
channel is close to what Lewis and Clark saw, and
Jefferson Landing at the foot of the capitol building is
one of the country's few remaining nineteenth-century
riverboat landings.

4

JUNE 17, 1804

George Drewyer our hunter and one man came in with 2 Deer & a Bear, also a young Horse, they had found in the Prarie, this horse has been in the Prarie a long time and is fat, I suppose he has been left by Some war party against the Osage, *This is a Crossing place for the war partis against that nation from the* Saukees, Aiaouez, *&* Souix. *The party is much aflicted with* boils *and Several have the Decissentary, which I contribute to the water*

The Countrey about this place is butifull   on the river & well timbered   on the S. S. about two miles back a Prarie coms. . . . well watered and abounds in De[e]r Elk & Bear. The Ticks & Musquetors are verry troublesom. —WILLIAM CLARK

This hiking and biking trail was built on the former corridor of the Kansas-Missouri-Texas Railroad, which ceased operation between Machens and Sedalia in 1986. The abandoned railroad bed was transformed into 185 miles of trails across the state of Missouri following the old train route. In the background is Interstate 70 as it crosses over the river.

4

KATY Trail and Missouri River, near Rocheport, Missouri

5

confluence of the
Kansas River with the
Missouri, Kansas City,
Missouri

JUNE 29, 1804

Ordered

a Court martial will Set this day at 11 oClock, to Consist of five members, for the trial of John Collins and Hugh Hall, Confined on Charges exhibited against them by Sergeant Floyd, agreeable to the articles of War. . . .

The Court Convened agreeable to order and proceeded to the trial of the Prisoners Viz John Collins Charged "with getting drunk on his post this morning out of whiskey put under his Charge as a Sentinal and for Suffering Hugh Hall to draw whiskey out of the Said Barrel intended for the party"

To this Charge the prisoner plead not guilty.

The Court after mature deliveration on the evidence abduced &c. are of oppinion that the prisoner is guilty of the Charge exibited against him, and do therefore Sentence him to recive one hundred lashes on his bear back.

Hugh Hall was brought [before the court and charged] with ["]takeing whiskey out of a Keg this morning which whiskey was Stored on the Bank (and under the Charge of the guard) Contrary to all order, rule, or regulation"

To this Charge the prisoner "Pleades Guilty."

The Court find the prisoner guilty and Sentence him to receive fifty Lashes on his bear Back.

The Commanding Officers approve of the Sentence of the Court and orders that the Punishment take place at half past three this evening, at which time the party will Parrade for inspection —WILLIAM CLARK

After traveling thirty-four days and four hundred river miles, the expedition reached the point where the Missouri River ends its westerly course and turns north, continuing about 1,100 miles almost to the Canadian border. The Corps spent about four days here, drying out wet supplies from the heavy rains, sunning, taking observations, and repacking goods. Lewis weighed the water from the two rivers and found the Missouri's to be heavier (it carried more mud) and to taste better. Clark also observed that it was "a butifull place for a fort, good landing place, the waters of the Kansas is verry disigreeably tasted to me." The photograph was taken from the same high point of land as Clark's good site for a fort, now in downtown Kansas City.

AUGUST 3, 1804

*mad[e] up a Small preasent for those people in perpo-
tion to their Consiqunce. also a package with a mead-
ile to accompany a Speech for the Grand Chief   after
Brackfast we Collected those Indians under an orning
of our Main Sail, in presence of our Party paraded &
Delivered a long Speech to them expressive of our
journey the wirkes of our Government, Some advice
to them and Directions how They were to Conduct
themselves, the princapal Chief for the nation being
absente we sent him the Speech <u>flag</u> Meadel & Some
Cloathes. after hering what they had to say Delivered
a medal of Second Grade to one for the Ottos & and
one for the Missourie present and 4 medals of a third
Grade to the inferior Chief   two for each tribe. . . .*

*Those Chiefs all Delivered a Speech acknowledge-
ing Their approbation to the Speech and promissing
to prosue the advice & Derictions given them   that
they wer happy to find that they had fathers which
might be depended on &c. We gave them a Cannister
of Powder and a Bottle of whiskey and delivered a
few presents to the whole after giveing a <u>br: cth:</u>
[breech cloth] Some Paint guartering & a Meadele to
those we <u>made</u> Cheifs* —WILLIAM CLARK

The expedition made camp near what is now Dodge
Park. It was a few days before their first meeting with
western Indian tribes. At their initial encounter with
the Oto and Missouri, the captains set the pattern for
future contacts: The Corps of Discovery paraded in
military formation and fired guns in unison. Then
Lewis and Clark displayed their technological won-
ders—magnets, compasses, and a magnifying glass that
could start a fire. For an impressive show of artillery,
Lewis fired an air-powered rifle that could sever a small
tree trunk. Next the captains made a long speech of
some 2,500 words, which took a half-hour to deliver,
including the translator. Clark spoke about the Indians'
great father in Washington who was sincerely con-
cerned about their well-being and who promised to
provide for all their needs as soon as he knew what they
were. Their new father set one condition, however: he
expected the tribes to stop their wars with each other.
As the ceremony drew to a close, the captains offered
token gifts of peace medals, paint, needles, and scissors
to the Indians who they determined were the chiefs.
They left with a final and stern warning: If the Indians
did not do as instructed, the great father in Washington
would stop all trade from coming up the river.

6

campsite, dodge park,
omaha, nebraska

{13}

7

AUGUST 18, 1804

a fine morning. Wind from the S. E. in the after part of the Day the Party with the Indians arrivd. we meet them under a Shade near the Boat and after a Short talk we gave them Provisions to eat & proceeded to the trail of Reed, he Confessed that he "Deserted & Stold a public Rifle Shot-pouch Powder & Bals" and requested we would be as favourable with him as we Could consistantly with our Oathes—which we were and only Sentenced him to run the Gantlet four times through the Party & that each man with 9 Swichies Should punish him and for him not to be considered in future as one of the Party—

The three principal Chiefs petitioned for Pardin for this man

After we explained the injurey Such men could doe them by false representation, & explang. the Customs of our Countrey they were all Satisfied with the propriety of the Sentence & was witness to the punishment. after which we had Some talk with the Chiefs about the orrigan of the war between them & the Mahars &c. &c.—.... Cap L. Birth day....

the evening was Closed with an extra Gill of Whiskey & a Dance untill 11 oClock.

—WILLIAM CLARK

Near Council Bluffs Private Moses B. Reed had received permission to go back downstream to retrieve his knife (a valuable tool on the frontier), but three days passed without his return. Faced with their first desertion, the captains sent four men to retrieve him, with orders to shoot if he resisted. Ten days later the men brought Reed back to stand trial.

Lewis designed and oversaw construction of the original keelboat in Pittsburgh, Pennsylvania. The boat builder's drunkenness led to repeated delays, and while Lewis was furious, he had no alternative but to wait. Fifty-five feet long and eight feet wide, the boat had a cargo capacity of twelve tons, with a cabin in the stern, a swivel gun at the bow, and a mast thirty-five feet high. The crew had to move it down the Ohio River to the Mississippi and then upstream to St. Louis; because of the delays the Ohio was difficult to navigate as the water level had dropped a great deal during the summer.

The boat moved by different means of propulsion: by pole pushing, where the men set long poles in the riverbed and then walked the length of the deck thereby pushing the boat forward; by rowing, with crew positions for twenty-two men; by sailing, when winds were favorable; and by pulling a long rope, with the men either on shore or wading in the water.

Clark determined that the best way to load the boat was to make it bow-heavy in order to bump directly into the many submerged logs floating down the Missouri rather than ride over the top of them. The keelboat was too large and heavy to go beyond the Mandan villages in North Dakota; the smaller pirogues were for the remaining journey west. Modern estimates for the total weight of the expedition's cargo are nearly thirty tons.

Among the items on Meriwether Lewis's packing list for the trip were: 3 thermometers; 2 "Artifical Horizons"; 6 "papers of Ink powder"; numerous books, maps, and charts; 45 rifles, 200 pounds of rifle powder, 400 pounds of lead, 15 "Powder Horns & pouches complete," and 15 "Pairs of Bullet Moulds"; 24 tomahawks; 24 large knives; 500 "best Flints"; 15 pairs of woolen overalls; 6 copper kettles; 2 vices; 2 "Vials of Phosforus"; 4 "Tin blowing Trumpets"; 20 yards "Strong Oznaburgs"; 24 iron spoons; "Muscatoe Curtains"; 150 pounds "Portable Soup"; and 1 "Sea Grass Hammock." The single most valuable item was a chronometer valued at $250.

He also brought with him 5,555 rations of flour, 4,000 rations of salt pork, 120 gallons of whiskey, tobacco, barrels of hog lard, and 3 bushels of rock salt. Among the medicinal treatments he thought to pack were 15 pounds of "Best powder's Bark," Epsom salts, opium, powdered rhubarb, white vitriol, a pound of "blistering ointments," and "flour of sulphur."

For the Indians, there were beads, scissors, thimbles, paint and vermilion, knives, combs, armbands, medals, and earrings. Jefferson sent two metal corn grinders as a special gift to the Mandan nation. In all, twenty-five bales of Indian goods were packed. Clark wrote of these goods as they departed that they were "such articles of merchandise as we thought ourselves authorized to procure—though not as much as I think necessary for the multitude of Indians through which we must pass on our road across the continent."

9

crumbling river bank
along the missouri,
near vermillion,
south dakota

AUGUST 5, 1804

Set out early   great appearance of wind and rain (I have observed that Thundor & lightning is not as common in this Countrey as it is in the atlantic States)   Snakes are not plenty, one was killed to day large and resembling the rattle Snake only Something lighter —. I walked on Shore this evening S. S. in Pursueing Some Turkeys I [s]truck the river twelve miles below within 370 yards, the high water passes thro this Peninsulia; and agreeable to the Customary Changes of the river I Concld. . . . that in two years the main Current of the river will pass through. In every bend the banks are falling in from the Current being thrown against those bends by the Sand points which inlarges and the Soil I believe from unquestionable appearns. of the entire bottom from one hill to the other being the mud or ooze of the River at Some former Period mixed with Sand and Clay easily melts and Slips into the River, and the mud mixes with the water & the Sand is washed down and lodges on the points — Great quantites of Grapes on the banks, I observe three different Kinds at this time ripe, one Of the no. is large & has the flaver of the Purple grape. camped on the S. S. the Musquitors verry troubleson. He man who went back after his Knife has not yet come up, we have Some reasons to believe he has Deserted —WILLIAM CLARK

As it runs on its long journey to the Gulf of Mexico, the Missouri slowly washes away the Rocky Mountains and leaves along the lower Missouri a mixture of clay and sandy soil. In spite of trees and low vegetation growing along these banks, trying to hold the soil together, the banks continue to crumble away into the river, washing downstream into the Gulf. This view is of one of the few sections of original riverbed, and is not part of the extensive, constructed channel that today contains and tries to control the bank erosion of the lower Missouri.

9

Sergeant Floyd much weaker and no better. . . .
Serjeant Floyd as bad as he can be   no pulse & noth-
ing will Stay a moment on his Stomach or bowels—

   Serj.' Floyd Died with a great deel of Composure,
before his death he Said to me, "I am going away . . .
I want you to write me a letter"— We buried him on
the top of the bluff ½ Miles below a Small river to
which we Gave his name, he was buried with the
Honors of War much lamented. . . . This Man at all
times gave us proofs of his firmness and Deturmined
resolution to doe Service to his Countrey and honor to
himself   after paying all the honor to our Decesed
brother we Camped in the mouth of Floyds *river*
about 30 yards wide, a butifull evening.

—WILLIAM CLARK

Despite countless incidents that could have resulted in
death, only one man died during the expedition—a
truly remarkable achievement. Sergeant Charles Floyd
died of a ruptured appendix; even the best medicine of
his time couldn't have saved him. On the return trip his
grave was discovered partially opened. Much later, in
1810, Clark reported that a Sioux chief had opened the
grave to place his son's body beside Floyd's, believing
the "next world" of the white man was happier than
that of the "Savages." The grave was moved more than
once because of the riverbank's erosion. What would
have been the original site now lies seventy feet in the
air above the Missouri.

IO

Floyd River
and abandoned
stockyards, sioux
city, iowa

II

AUGUST 24, 1804

Capt Lewis and my Self Concluded to visit a High Hill Situated in an emence Plain three Leagues N. 20° W. from the mouth of White Stone river, this hill appear to be of a Conic form and by all the different Nations in this quater is Supposed to be a place of Deavels or that they are in human form with remarkable large heads and about 18 inches high; that they are very watchfull and ar armed with Sharp arrows with which they can kill at a great distance; they are said to kill all persons who are so hardy as to attemp to approach the hill; they state that tradition informs them that ma[n]y indians have suffered by these little people and among others that three Maha men fell a sacrefice to their murceyless fury not meany years since—so much do the Mahas Souix Ottoes and other neibhbouring nations believe this fable that no consideration is sufficient to induce them to approach this hill. —WILLIAM CLARK

This small, conical mound of grassy earth is about fifty feet higher than the surrounding country, with a distinct point at the top, and it is one of the few places where one can stand today and be certain that Lewis and Clark also stood there. The captains hiked the eight miles from the river and reported buffalo herds as far as the eye could see. Lewis could barely make the hike up to the mound, as he was suffering from the effects of breathing cobalt and arsenic vapors in his attempts to identify the substances.

a verry Cold morning   Set out at day light   we landed after proceding 5½ miles, near the foot of a round mounting which I saw yesterday resembling a dome.

Capt Lewis & my Self walked up, to the top which forms a Cone and is about 70 feet higher than . . . the high lands around it, the Bass is about 300 foot   in decending this Cupola, discovered a Village of Small animals that burrow in the grown (those animals are Called by the french Pitite Chien)   Killed one & Cought one a live by poreing a great quantity of water in his hole   we attempted to dig to the beds of one of thos animals, after diging 6 feet, found by running a pole down that we were not half way to his Lodges, we found 2 frogs in the hole, and killed a Dark rattle Snake near with a Ground rat . . . in him, (those rats are numerous)   the Village of those animals Covs. about 4 acrs of Ground on a Gradual decent of a hill and Contains great numbers of holes on the top of which those little animals Set erect make a Whistleing noise and whin allarmed Slip into their hole— we por'd into one of the holes 5 barrels of water without filling it, Those Animals are about the Size of a Small Squrel . . . & thicker, the head much resembling a Squirel in every respect, except the ears

which is Shorter, his tail like a ground Squirel which thy Shake & whistle when allarmd. the toe nails long, they have fine fur & the longer hair is gray, it is Said that a kind of Lizard also a Snake reside with those animals. . . . Camped —WILLIAM CLARK

Looming above the rolling prairies, Mount Baldy can be seen from some distance on the river. The Corps of Discovery hiked to Baldy, where they discovered a small, furry, doglike animal—what we call prairie dogs. This "site location" of the North American prairie dog is on private property and not easily accessible.

Mount Baldy, near Gross, Nebraska

13

New bridge construction,
Niobrara, Nebraska

AUGUST 29, 1804

*Some rain last night & this morning. . . . at 4 oClock
P M. Sergt. Pryor & Mr. Dorion with 5 chiefs and
about 70 men . . . arrived on the opposite Side   we
Sent over a Perogue & Mr. Dorrion & his Son who
was tradeing with the Indians Came over with Serjt
Pryer, and informed us that the Chiefs were there
we Sent Serjt. Pryor & yound Mr. Dorion with Som
Tobacco, Corn & a few Kittles for them to Cook in,
with directions to inform the Chiefs that we would
Speek to them tomorrow.*

   *Serjt. Pryor informs me that when Came near the
Indian Camp they were met by men with a Buffalow
roabe to Carry them, Mr. Dorion informed [them
that] ["]they were not the Owners of the Boats & did
not wish to be Carried"— the Sceoüex Camps are
handson of a Conic form Covered with Buffalow
Roabs Painted different Colours and all Compact &
hand Somly arranged, covered all round an orpen
part in the Center for the fire, with Buffalow roabs
each Lodg has a place for Cooking detached, the
lodges contain 10 to 15 persons — a Fat Dog was
presented as a mark of their Great respect for the
party of which they partook hartily and thought it
good & well flavored* —WILLIAM CLARK

The expedition was approaching the land of the Sioux
Indians. On Jefferson's order, Lewis and Clark were to
win the Sioux's respect for Washington's power and to
instruct them to stop warring with other tribes. The
Sioux routinely demanded heavy tribute from river
travelers, and had been denying passage to traders from
St. Louis who were trying to reach the Mandan villages
in North Dakota. As Jefferson knew, peace and safe
passage were prerequisites for productive commerce.

   There were two bands of Sioux: the relatively
peaceful Yankton, who were located near what is now
Niobrara, and the hostile Teton, who lived closer to
the Canadian border. The Yankton Sioux traded
sporadically with St. Louis merchants, and Lewis
and Clark encountered them first. The Tetons traded
with the British in the Lake Winnipeg region and
fiercely protected their power on the upper Missouri.
They harassed traders who came into their territory
and terrorized neighboring tribes. Jefferson found
this situation unacceptable, and the captains intended
to alter it.

AUGUST 30, 1804

*a verry thick fog this morning   after Prepareing
Some presents for the Chiefs which we <made> . . .
and finishing a Speech . . . we Sent Mr. Dorion in a
Perogue for the Chiefs & warreirs to a Council under
an Oak tree near wher we had a flag flying on a high
flag Staff   at 12 OClock we met and Cap L.
Delivered the Speech & thin made one great Chiff by
giving him a meadal & Some Cloathes one 2 d. Chief
& three third Chiefs in the Same way, They recvd.
those thing with the goods and tobacco with pleasure
. . . we Smoked out of the pipe of peace*

AUGUST 31, 1804

*after the Indians got their Brackfast the Chiefs met
and arranged themselves in a row with elligent pipes
of peace all pointing to our Seets, we Came foward
and took our Seets, the Great Cheif <u>the shake han</u> rose
and Spoke to Some length aproving what we had
Said and promising to pursue the advice.*

*   last night the Indians Danced untill late   in their
dances we gave them Som knives Tobaco & belts &
tape & Binding with which they wer Satisfied*

—WILLIAM CLARK

This wide river channel is the beginning of a five-hundred-mile-long lake through the Dakotas created by a
series of six dams and the gentle down slope of the
Missouri River through the Great Plains. Near here is
Calumet Bluff, site of Lewis and Clark's first council
with the Yankton Sioux. The travelers set the prairie on
fire in two places to signal their desire for a council, and
they camped on Calumet Bluff, awaiting the arrival of
the Indians. Lewis, with the help of an interpreter,
delivered what became his typical speech. Chief
Weuche agreed to go to Washington in the spring to
meet the "Great Father," and several other chiefs made
short speeches asking for powder, ball, and liquor;
instead, they were given trinkets.

16

15

SEPTEMBER 16, 1804

*we sent three hunters out who soon added eight deer
and two Buffaloe to our strock of provisions; the
Buffaloe were so pour that we took only the tongues
skins and marrow bones; the skins were particularly
acceptable as we were in want of a covering for the
large perogue to secure the baggage*

SEPTEMBER 17, 1804

*this senery already rich pleasing and beatiful, was still
farther hightened by immence herds of Buffaloe deer
Elk and Antelopes which we saw in every direction
feeding on the hills and plains. I do not think I ex-
agerate when I estimate the number of Buffaloe which
could be compreed at one view to amount to 3000.*

MAY 5, 1805

*we kill whatever we wish, the buffaloe furnish us with
fine veal and fat beef, we also have venison and beaver
tales when we wish them; the flesh of the Elk and
goat are less esteemed, and certainly are inferior. . . .
saw the carcases of many Buffaloe lying dead along
the shore partially devoured by the wolves and bear.*

—MERIWETHER LEWIS

On August 23, 1804, Private Joseph Field killed the expedition's first buffalo at a site not far from present-day Sioux City, Iowa. That evening the men ate their first meal of buffalo hump, tongue, and steaks. While they were on the Plains, buffalo was the Corps' principal source of food, and the men liked eating buffalo hump and tongue better than anything except beaver tail. The French traders were the only men with the expedition who had seen buffalo before.

SEPTEMBER 17, 1804

*Having for many days past confined myself to the
boat, I determined to devote this day to amuse myself
on shore with my gun and view the interior of the
country lying between the river and the Corvus
Creek— accordingly before sunrise I set out with six
of my best hunters. . . . one quarter of a mile in rear
of our camp which was situated in a fine open grove
of cotton wood passed a grove of plumb trees loaded
with fruit and now ripe. observed but little difference
between this fruit and that of a similar kind common
to the Atlantic States. . . . this forrest of plumb trees
garnish a plain about 20 feet more lelivated than that
on which we were encamped. . . . and is intirely occu-
pyed by the burrows of the barking squril hertefore
discribed; this anamal appears here in infinite numbers, and the shortness and virdue [verdure] of grass
gave the plain the appearance throughout it's whole
extent of beatifull bowlinggreen. . . . a great number
of wolves of the small kind, halks and some pole-cats
were to be seen. I presume that those anamals feed on
this squirril.* —MERIWETHER LEWIS

As they passed through here, the Corps discovered a
natural paradise of animal and plant life in an ecosys-
tem that had existed for centuries. A month earlier, on
August 16, Clark had reported in his journal that Lewis
and twelve men had gone fishing in a pond and creek
and caught "about 800 fine fish . . . 79 Pike, 8 Salmon,
1 Rock, 1 flat Back, 127 Buffalow & readhorse, 4 Bass,
and 490 Cat, with many Small & large Silver fish and
shrimp." Today immense fields of sunflowers grow
along the Missouri corridor in the Dakotas, thriving on
the available river water and flourishing in the prairie
soil and warm sun.

16

sunflower crop,
Lower Brule Sioux
Indian Reservation,
South Dakota

SEPTEMBER 11, 1804

thus a man had like to have Starved to death in a land of Plenty for the want of Bulletes or Something to kill his meat —WILLIAM CLARK

The men often traveled separately. Lewis took long walks alone, sometimes going as far as thirty miles in a day, collecting plant specimens. Individual hunters also headed out into the countryside in search of game. Near Lake Oahe nineteen-year-old George Shannon, the youngest member of the Corps, failed to return from hunting. After the men searched but did not find him, they feared he had come upon Indian trouble or suffered an accident. Twelve days later, as the keelboat rounded a bend, the crew spotted Shannon sitting on the river-bank. He thought that the boats were ahead of him and had been chasing them, when in fact, he was in the lead. By September 11, he had grown too weak to continue his chase. He had no more bullets, and was sitting by the river hoping to catch a ride back to St. Louis on a trading boat. While lost, Shannon had turned a short stick into a bullet and killed a rabbit, but mostly he sur-vived on the wild plums and grapes he found growing along the way.

17

Lake Oahe and the Missouri River, South Dakota

18

antelope creek at
missouri river, near
pierre, south dakota

*passed a Small Creek on the S. S. 16 yds wide   I call
<u>Reubens</u> Cr.— R. Fields was the first who found it —
Came too & Camped on the S. S. in a Wood. Soon
after we landed three <u>Soues</u> boys Swam across to us,
those boys informed us that a Band of Sieux called the
<u>Tetons</u> of 80 Lodges wer Camped near the mouth of
the next River, and 60 Lodges more a Short distance
above them, they had that day Set the praries on fire to
let those Camps Know of our approach — we gave
those boys two twists of Tobacco to carry to their Chiefs
& Warriors to Smoke, with derections to tell them that
we wished to Speak to them tomorrow, at the mouth of
the next river.* —WILLIAM CLARK

The party was rapidly approaching Teton Sioux country.
Propelled by strong fall winds from the south, the keel-
boat covered almost seventy-five miles in three days.
The Corps was at the mouth of what is now called
Antelope Creek when the three boys came to visit.

19

SEPTEMBER 25, 1804

I went with those Cheifs . . . in one of the Perogues with 5 men . . . to Shore with a view of reconseleing those men to us, as Soon as I landed the Perogue three of their young men Seased the Cable of the Perogue . . . in which we had presents . . . the Chiefs Soldr . . . Huged the mast, and the 2d Chief was verry insolent both in words & justures . . . declareing I Should not go on, Stateing he had not recved presents Suffient from us, his justures were of Such a personal nature I felt my Self Compeled to Draw my Sword . . . and made a Signal to the boat to prepar for action at this motion Capt. Lewis ordered all under arms in the boat, those with me also Showed a Disposition to Defend themselves and me, the grand Chief then took hold of the roop & ordered the young warrers away . . .

    Most of the warriers appeared to have ther Bows Strung and took out their arrows from ther quves. as I . . . being surrounded was not permited . . . by them . . . to return, I Sent all the men except 2 Inpt. [interpreters] to the boat, the perogu Soon returned with about 12 of our detumind men ready for any event this movement . . . caused a no: of the Indians to withdraw at a distance . . . <u>leaving their chiefs soldiers alone with me</u>   Their treatment to me was verry rough & I think justified roughness on my part . . .

we proceeded on about 1 mile & anchored out off a willow Island placed a guard on Shore to protect the Cooks & a guard in the boat, fastened the Perogues to the boat, I call this Island bad humered Island as we were in a bad humer. —WILLIAM CLARK

Well aware of potential trouble from the Teton Sioux, the expedition anchored off shore at the mouth of what was then called the Teton River. The name was changed to Bad River later in the nineteenth century. The men stayed on their boats, with guards stationed on shore. Nine hundred Teton Sioux were also camped here. For a few days they treated the travelers with hospitality, even performing two scalp dances late at night to celebrate their recent killing of Omaha Indians and the capture of forty-eight Omaha women and children. But their mood changed to hostility when the captains offered them cheap medals and trinkets instead of guns and whiskey. Fearing an attack, Lewis loaded the swivel gun with sixteen musket balls, lighted a taper, and took aim at the Teton Sioux while the other men loaded blunderbusses with buckshot. The chiefs, believing the captains would fight to the death over "trinkets," called off their warriors. They knew that even if they did win the battle their losses would be significant. For the first time the Teton Sioux failed to extract their usual tribute from river travelers.

The Souix is a Stout bold looking people, (the young men hand Som) & well made, the greater part of them make use of Bows & arrows, Some fiew fusees I observe among them, not with Standing they live by the Bow & arrow, they do not Shoot So well as the Northern Indians   the Warriers are Verry much deckerated with Paint Porcupin quils & feathers, large leagins & mockersons, all with buffalow roabs of Different Colours. the Squars wore Peticoats & and a white Buffalow roabes with the black hair turned back over their necks & Sholders

I will here remark a Society which I had never before this day heard was in any nation of Indians — four of which is at this time present and all who remain of this Band — Those who become members of this Society must be brave active young men who take a <u>Vow</u> never to give back let the danger be what it may; in War Parties they always go forward without Screening themselves behind trees or any thing else to this Vow they Strictly adheer dureing their Lives
—WILLIAM CLARK

The Hunkpapa Sioux are the tribe of the legendary Chief Sitting Bull, who was killed in 1890 at Fort Yates on Standing Rock Indian Reservation. Though a monument at the fort commemorates his death, his body rests in a grave near Mobridge, North Dakota. Fort Yates is now a town on the reservation.

20

Hunkpapa Sioux
Indian boys,
Fort Yates,
North Dakota

SEPTEMBER 21, 1804

at half past one oClock this morning the Sand bar on which we Camped began to under mind and give way which allarmed the Sergeant on Guard, the motion of the boat awakened me; I get up & by the light of the moon observed that the land had given away both above and below our Camp & was falling in fast. I ordered all hands on as quick as possible & pushed off, we had pushed off but a few minets before the bank under which the Boat & perogus lay give way, which would Certainly have Sunk both Perogues, by the time we made the opsd. Shore our Camp fell in

—WILLIAM CLARK

To ensure their safety from Indians, the men would often camp on a sandbar for the night, sometimes not very successfully or comfortably. The sand bars shifted daily, proving a constant danger to the expedition as they navigated the river.

Bismarck,
North Dakota

22

sacred rock of the
mandans, near fort
clark, north dakota

According to legend, a giant turtle came out of the river to protect and advise the Mandans; it never returned to the river but instead became the sacred rock. Moments before the end of the world all the Mandan people will gather at the rock and sing. While they are singing, the rock will once again become a turtle and protect the tribe. A sign of the impending Armaggedon is the rock's cracking, which began with a small fissure in 1984. The rock is now separated into three giant pieces. Long before this happened, the Mandans suffered a different kind of armaggedon—smallpox. An outbreak in 1781 reduced the population dramatically; after the 1837 epidemic, fewer than 150 Mandans survived. The sacred rock is not only a reminder of what might have been, but also of what has been. The North Dakota highway department moved Turtle Rock from a nearby ridge top and placed it at a scenic turnoff on State Highway 200 in the early 1980s.

northern prairie grass,
fort berthold indian
reservation, near white
shield, north dakota

OCTOBER 29, 1804

The Prarie was Set on fire (or Cought by accident) by a young man of the Mandins, the fire went with Such velocity that it burnt to death a man and woman, who Could not Get to any place of Safty, one man a woman & Child much burnt and Several narrowly escaped the flame — a boy half white was Saved un hurt in the midst of the flaim, Those ignerent people Say this boy was Saved by the great Spirit medisin because he was white — The Cause of his being Saved was a Green buffalow Skin was thrown over him by his mother who perhaps had more fore Sight for the pertection of her . . . Son, and [l]ess for herself than those who escaped the flame, the Fire did not burn under the Skin leaving the grass round the boy

—WILLIAM CLARK

From St. Louis to the Rocky Mountains in central Montana, the Missouri River meanders through the Great Plains for some two thousand miles. All around the travelers were vast grasslands. Clark commented in his journals on the changing character of the grass, which was six-feet high on the lower Missouri but was much shorter when they reached the northern prairie.

NOVEMBER 30, 1804

This morning at 8 oClock an Indian Calld from the other Side and informed that he had Something of Consequence to Communicate. we Sent a perogue for him & he informed us as follows. Viz: "five men of the Mandan Nation out hunting in a S. W. derection about Eight Leagues was Suprised by a large party of Sceoux & Panies, one man was Killed and two wounded with arrows & 9 Horses taken, 4 of the We ter Soon nation [the Awaxawi Hidatsas] was missing, & they expected to be attacked by the Souix. . . . we thought it well to Show a Disposition to ade and assist them against their enemies, perticularly those who Came in oppersition to our Councils, . . . I crossed the river in about an hour after the arrival of the Indian express with 23 men including the inter-peters. . . . The Indians not expecting . . . to receive Such Strong aide in So Short a time was much Suprised, and a littled allarmed at the formadable appearance of my party—

I then informed them that if they would assemble their warrers and those of the different Towns I would to meet the Army of Souix & Chastise thim for take-ing the blood of our dutifull Children &c. after a conversation of a fiew minits anongst themselves, one Chief the big man cien . . . Said they now Saw that what we hade told them was the trooth, whin we expected the enimies of their Nation was Comeing to attact them, or had spilt their blood [we] were ready to protect them, and Kill those who would not listen to our Good talk. —WILLIAM CLARK

The men spent the winter of 1804–05 in a fortification that they constructed and named Fort Mandan. By November 1804 the expedition had traveled 1,609 miles, all upstream. Lewis and Clark chose the site for their winter quarters because there was a wealth of cottonwood trees for building, and it was also close to the Indian villages on the opposite shore. Although the original site of the fort has vanished, it is believed to be near the center of the view in this photograph.

During the long winter Lewis and Clark exhaustively studied their neighbors—the Mandan and Hidatsa Indians, some four thousand in number. They hoped to convince the Mandans that Washington would protect them, a strategy intended to eliminate the influence of British traders. Despite Clark's willingness to protect the Mandans, the snow was so deep the men could not ride their horses and so failed to carry off the promised revenge raids on the Sioux and Pawnees.

When spring arrived the captains reduced the Corps' numbers, sending men back to St. Louis with the large keelboat and their journals and notes as well as many plant and animal specimens.

24

site of fort Mandan, near washburn, North Dakota

25

25

Arc of the Lone Man and replica of a Mandan earth lodge, Fort Abraham Lincoln, North Dakota

Whether this medicine was truly the cause or not I shall not undertake to determine, but I was informed that she had not taken it more than ten minutes before she brought forth   perhaps this remedy may be worthy of future experiments, but I must confess that I want faith as to it's efficacy. —MERIWETHER LEWIS

During the particularly cold winter of 1804–05 —the temperature averaged four degrees above zero— Sacagawea, a fourteen-year-old war captive, and her owner and husband, a French trader, Toussaint Charbonneau, were added to the party to act as interpreters on the recommendation of the Mandans. Sacagawea, Lewis and Clark believed, would be especially useful because Shoshone was her native tongue; the expedition would need to obtain horses from the Shoshone Indians when they reached the Rocky Mountains.

Lewis, who traded his doctoring skills to the Mandan for corn, assisted in treating Sacagawea with a drink of rattlesnake rattles mixed with water to ease her labor in giving birth to her son. Lewis doubted the value of this potion as well as other medical treatments he provided, but without having something to trade the Corps would not have survived the winter. As buffalo had migrated out to the plains and were scarce, the Indians' stock of corn proved essential. Doctoring was one way to barter, but even more important for trade were the skills of Private John Shields. Shields was a blacksmith and earned trade credits by mending hoes and axes and repairing firearms for the Indians. Fortunately, he discovered that he could also make Indian battle axes, a new product to barter—so popular were these weapons that Shields cut up an old cooking stove to make more. One ax could fetch seven or eight gallons of corn. In this trade both sides thought they made the better bargain.

JANUARY 5, 1805

a Buffalow Dance (or Medison) . . . for 3 nights passed in the 1st Village, a curious Custom the old men arrange themselves in a circle & after Smoke a pipe, which is handed them by a young man, Dress up for the purpose, the young men who have their wives back of the circle . . . go to one of the old men with a whining tone and . . . <request> the old man to take his wife (who presents necked except a robe) and—(or Sleep with him)   the Girl then takes the Old man (who verry often can Scercely walk) and leads him to a Convenient place for the business, after which they return to the lodge, if the Old man (or a white man) returns to the lodge without gratifying the man & his wife, he offers her again and again; it is often the Case that after the 2d time <he> without Kissing the Husband throws a nice robe over the old man & and begs him not to dispise him, & his wife

(we Sent a man to this Medisan <Dance> last night, they gave him 4 Girls)

all this is to cause the buffalow to Come near So that They may kill thim —WILLIAM CLARK

The Indians and Corps of Discovery danced and played music for each other. The Indians were fascinated by the fiddle, tambourine, and sounding horn and greatly amused by the dancing of Clark's slave, York, who danced very fast. François Rivet, a Frenchman, had another entertaining trick—he could dance on his hands.

26

Mandan Indian dancers,
Fort Abraham Lincoln,
North Dakota

27

JANUARY 10, 1804

last night was excessively Cold the murkery this morning Stood at 40° below 0 which is 72° below the freesing point, we had one man out last night, who returned about 8 oClock this morning The Indians of the lower Villages turned out to hunt for a man & a boy who had not returnd from the hunt of yesterday, and borrowd a Slay to bring them in expecting to find them frosed to death about 10 oclock the boy about 13 years of age Came to the fort with his feet frosed and had layen out last night without fire with only a Buffalow Robe to Cover him, the Dress which he wore was a pr of . . . Legins, which is verry thin and mockersons — we had his feet put in Cold water and they are Comeing too — Soon after the arrival of the Boy, a man Came in who had also Stayed out without fire, and verry thinly Clothed, this man was not the least injured —

Customs & the habits of those people has ancered to bare more Cold than I thought it possible for man to indure —

JANUARY 27, 1804

a fine day, attempt to Cut our Boat and canoes out of the ice, a deficuelt Task I fear as we find waters between the Ice, I Bleed the man with the Plurisy to day & Swet him, Capt Lewis took of the Toes of one foot of the Boy who got frost bit Some time ago
—WILLIAM CLARK

According to recent research, the nearest Mandan Indian village, called "1st Mandan Village" by Lewis and Clark, was some two miles upriver from Fort Mandan. In 1974, the National Park Service established the 1,758-acre Knife River Indian Villages National Historic Site and carried on an intensive archaeological survey that resulted in over fifty archaeological sites, recording some 8,000 years of habitation by the northern Plains Indians. Archaeologists were able to identify the presence of settlements by the Hidatsa and Mandan Indians during the final five hundred years of this long period. These were the native peoples encountered by the Corps in the neighborhood of Fort Mandan. Today the village, known to the Indians as "Big White's" village, lies beneath the Leland Olds Station of the Basin Electric Power Cooperative.

27

28

On to the Pacific

APRIL 7, 1805

Our vessels consisted of six small canoes, and two large perogues. This little fleet altho' not quite so rispectable as those of Columbus or Capt. Cook were still viewed by us with as much pleasure as those deservedly famed adventurers ever beheld theirs; and I dare say with quite as much anxiety for their safety and preservation. we were now about to penetrate a country at least two thousand miles in width, on which the foot of civillized man had never trodden; the good or evil it had in store for us was for experiment yet to determine, and these little vessells contained every article by which we were to expect to subsist or defend ourselves. . . . entertaining as I do, the most confident hope of succeading in a voyage which had formed a da[r]ling project of mine for the last ten years, I could but esteem this moment of my departure as among the most happy of my life. —MERIWETHER LEWIS

As soon as the ice broke, early in April 1805, the expedition left Fort Mandan. The Corps would be out of communication for more than a year. This photograph was made very near the site where the original fort stood.

APRIL 13, 1805

Being disappointed in my observations of yesterday for Longitude, I was unwilling to remain at the entrance of the river another day for that purpose, and therefore determined to set out early this morning; which we did accordingly; the wind was in our favour after 9 A.M. and continued favourable untill three 3 P.M. we therefore hoisted both the sails in the White Perogue, consisting of a small squar sail, and spritsail, which carried her at a pretty good gate, untill about 2 in the afternoon when a suddon squall of wind struck us and turned the perogue so much on the side as to allarm Sharbono who was steering at the time, in this state of alarm he threw the perogue with her side to the wind, when the spritsail gibing was as near overseting the perogue as it was possible to have missed. the wind however abating for an instant I ordered Drewyer to the helm and the sails to be taken in, which was instant executed and the perogue being steered before the wind was agin plased in a state of security. this accedent was very near costing us dearly. beleiving this vessell to be the most steady and safe, we had embarked on board of it our instruments, Papers, medicine and the most valuable part of the merchandize which we had still in reserve as presents for the Indians. we had also embarked on board ourselves, with three men who could not swim and the squaw with the young child, all of whom, had the perogue overset, would most probably have perished, as the waves were high, and the perogue upwards of 200 yards from the nearest shore

—MERIWETHER LEWIS

The only free-flowing section of the Missouri River that remains in North Dakota begins here at Garrison Dam and continues sixty miles downriver to Bismarck. The dam was built in 1953 to end the flooding of cities downstream, such as Omaha and Kansas City. Two miles long and two hundred feet high, this earth-filled dam dramatically altered two hundred miles of meandering river and turned it into massive Lake Sakakawea. The traditional North Dakotan spelling of Sacagawea's name is "Sakakawea" and reflects the belief that her name was of Hidatsa origin rather than Shoshone. In Hidatsa the word means "bird woman"; in Shoshone, "boat launcher." It was on the span of river now somewhere under Lake Sakakawea that the pirogue nearly turned over, one of the expedition's many near-accidents.

FROM THE LAST SPEECH OF FOUR BEARS, A GREAT MANDAN CHIEF, 1837

Ever since I can remember I have loved the whites. I have lived with them ever since I was a boy and to the best of my knowledge, I have never wronged a white man. On the contrary, I have always protected them from the insults of others, which they cannot deny. The Four Bears never saw a white man hungry, but what he gave them to eat, drink, and a buffalo skin to sleep on in time of need. I was always ready to die for them, which they cannot deny. I have done everything that a red skin could do for them, and how they have repaid it! With ingratitude! I have never called a white man a dog, but today I pronounce them to be a set of black-hearted dogs. The have deceived me. Them that I always considered as brothers have turned out to be my worst enemies.

I have been in many battles, and often wounded, but the wounds of my enemies I exult in. But today I am wounded, and by whom, by those same white dogs I have always considered and treated as brothers.

I do not fear death, my friends. You know it. But to die with my face rotten, that even the wolves will shrink with horror at seeing me, and say to themselves, "That is the Four Bears, the friend of the whites."

Listen well to what I have to say, as it will be the last time you will hear me. Think of your wives, children, brothers, sisters, friends, and in fact all that you hold dear. All are dead or dying, with their faces all rotten, caused by those dogs the whites. Think of all that, my friends, and rise together and not leave one of them alive.

New Town was established in the 1950s when the resevoir created by the Garrison Dam inundated seven towns, home to Mandan, Hidatsa, and Arikara Indians. The Indians' farms, located on bottomland, suffered the same fate, ending what had been a relatively self-sufficient native economy. All three displaced tribes are now blended together in the community of New Town. Their major source of income is the Four Bears Gambling Casino, named for the great chief who died from smallpox in 1837.

JULY 13, 1805

The Musquetoes and knats are more troublesome here if possible than they were at the White bear Islands. I sent a man to the canoes for my musquetoe bier which I had neglected to bring with me, as it is impossible to sleep a moment without being defended against the attacks of these most tormenting of all insects; the man returned with it a little after dark.

—MERIWETHER LEWIS

AUGUST 4, 1806

Musquetors excessively troublesome So much So that the men complained that they could not work at their Skins for those troublesom insects. and I find it entirely impossible to hunt in the bottoms, those insects being So noumerous and tormenting as to render it imposseable for a man to continue in the timbered lands and our best retreat from those insects is on the Sand bars in the river and even those Situations are only clear of them when the Wind Should happen to blow which it did to day for a fiew hours in the middle of the day. the evenings nights and mornings they are almost indureable perticelarly by the party with me who have no Bears to keep them off at night, and nothing to Screen them but their blankets which are worn and have maney holes. The torments of those Missquetors and the want of a Sufficety of Buffalow meat to dry, those animals not to be found in this neighbourhood induce me to deturmine to proceed on to a more eliagiable Spot on the Missouri below at which place the Musquetors will be less troublesom and Buffalow more plenty. . . . At 5 P. M. Set out and proceeded on down to the 2d point which appeared to be an eligable Situation for my purpose killed a porcupine on this point the Musquetors were So abundant that we were tormented much worst than at the point. The Child of Shabono has been So much bitten by the Musquetor that his face is much puffed up & Swelled. —WILLIAM CLARK

This mosquito-netted camper sits in the campsite that was used by the expedition on both its outbound and return journeys at what Lewis and Clark called "Stonewall Creek," today's Eagle Creek. For the Corps of Discovery mosquitoes were constant oppressors—at times they were so thick the hunters could not see to aim their rifles. The cliffs in the background are in the heart of the "Wild and Scenic White Cliffs," a much-visited area of the upper Missouri where commercial outfitters rent canoes and provisions for vacationers who then float down a hundred-mile stretch of protected waterway. Here a smooth and steady three-mile-an-hour current aids in the descent through the White Cliffs and beyond through the Missouri Breaks.

MAY 31, 1805

The hills and river Clifts which we passed today exhibit a most romantic appearance. The bluffs of the river rise to the hight of from 2 to 300 feet and in most places nearly perpendicular; they are formed of remarkable white sandstone which is Sufficiently soft to give way readily to the impression of water; two or three thin horizontal Stratas of white free Stone, on which the rains or water make no impression, lie imbeded in those clifts of Soft Stone near the upper part of them; the earth on the top of these clifts is a dark rich loam, which forming a gradual ascending plain extends back from ½ a mile to a mile where the hills commence and rise abruptly to a hight of about 300 feet more. The water in the Course of time acecending from those hills and plains on either side of the river has trickled down the Soft Sand Clifts and woarn it into a thousand grotesque figures; which with the help of a little imagination and an oblique view at a distance are made to represent elegant ranges of lofty freestone buildings, haveing their parapets well Stocked with Statuary; Collumns of various Sculptures both Grooved and plain, are also Seen Supporting long galleries in part of those buildings; in other places on a much nearer approach and with the . . . help of less immagination we See the remains of ruins of eligant buildings; Some Collumns Standing and almost entire with their pedestals and Capitals, others retaining their pedestals but deprived by time or accedint of their capitals, Some lying prostrate and broken, others in the form of vast pyramids of connic Structure bearing a serious of other pyramids on their tops becoming less as they ascend and finally termonateing in a sharp point. nitches and alcoves of various forms and Sizes are Seen at different hights as we pass.
—MERIWETHER LEWIS

On May 31, 1805, Lewis and Clark made camp in a grove of trees on the bank facing these two six-foot-high columns. Once connected by a delicate stone arch, these columns were a Montana landmark known as the Eye of the Needle. It is thought that vandals hiked up to this seemingly inaccessible point (some 150 feet straight up from the river) and used crowbars to dislodge the stone arch that until the summer of 1997 had firmly linked the two columns, forming a natural archway.

32

Broken Eye of the Needle, white cliffs, Montana

31

33

JUNE 7, 1805

It continued to rain almost without intermission last night . . . the ground remarkably slipry, insomuch that we were unable to walk on the sides of the bluffs where we had passed as we ascended the river. . . . In passing along the face of one of these bluffs today I sliped at a narrow pass of about 30 yards in length and but for a quick and fortunate recovery by means of my espontoon I should been precipitated into the river down a craggy pricipice of about ninety feet. I had scarcely reached a place on which I could stand with tolerable safety . . . before I heard a voice behind me cry out god god Capt. what shall I do   on turning about I found it was Windsor who had sliped and fallen abut the center of this narrow pass and was lying prostrate on his belley, with his . . . wright hand arm and leg over the precipice while he was holding on with the left arm and foot as well as he could which appeared to be with much difficulty. . . . I expected every instant to see him loose his strength and slip off; altho' much allarmed at his situation I disguised my feelings and spoke very calmly to him and assured him that he was in no kind of danger, to take the knife out of his belt behind him with his wright hand and dig a hole with it in the face of the bank to receive his wright foot which he did and then raised himself to his knees; I then directed him to take off his mockersons and to come forward on his hands and knees holding the knife in one hand and the gun in the other   this he happily effected and escaped
—MERIWETHER LEWIS

About midway across Montana the expedition encountered a major river entering the Missouri from the northwest. The Hidatsa Indians had been accurate about the many tributaries up to this point, but they had not mentioned this river. It looked equal in size and volume to the Missouri and had the same brown color and turbulent surface. The other fork's water was clear, swift, and placid.

The Corps spent nine days here trying to determine which fork to follow. Every man, including Private Cruzatte, an expert Missouri navigator, was convinced that the muddy branch was the Missouri and would lead straight to the mountains. Lewis and Clark believed the opposite; they understood the Louisiana Purchase to include all the drainage east of the Rocky Mountains and correctly surmised that the clear branch had come from the mountains and was the true Missouri River. The Hidatsas did not know the river for a simple reason—they raided west on horseback, taking shortcuts that never crossed its path. Lewis named the river after his cousin Maria Wood and led a four-day, seventy-seven-mile exploration of it, nearly losing a man on the slippery and saturated clay soil.

33

confluence of the Marias River with the Missouri, Loma, Montana

34

Road kill, Highway 12,
Santee Sioux Indian
Reservation, Nebraska

JULY 13, 1805

we eat an emensity of meat; it requires 4 deer, an Elk and a deer, or one buffaloe, to supply us plentifully 24 hours. meat now forms our food prinsipally as we reserve our flour parched meal and corn as much as possible for the rocky mountains which we are shortly to enter, and where from the indian account game is not very abundant. —MERIWETHER LEWIS

Each man consumed around six pounds of meat a day to balance their caloric output as they hauled the heavy boats upstream. Their health suffered from a diet limited almost entirely to meat and a little cornmeal. They had painful boils and lesions — and these problems persisted and worsened when berries and vegetables became scarce. (They had neglected to pack vinegar to mix with the drinking water to help prevent scurvy.)

MAY 31, 1805

The obstructions of rocky points and riffles still continue as yesterday; at those places the men are compelled to be in the water even to their armpits, and the water is yet very could, and so frequent are those point that they are one fourth of their time in the water, added to this the banks and bluffs along which they are obliged to pass are so slippery and the mud so tenacious that they are unable to wear their mockersons, and in that situation draging the heavy burthen of a canoe and walking ocasionally for several hundred yards over the sharp fragments of rocks which tumble from the clifts and garnish the borders of the river; in short their labour is incredibly painfull and great, yet those faithfull fellows bear it without a murmur.

—MERIWETHER LEWIS

By spring 1805 the expedition had coalesced in its purpose, and there were few serious discipline problems. Lewis and Clark now wrote more about the men's suffering from illnesses and difficulties of the journey. Dysentery was constant as were other assorted stomach ailments, and the men's feet were blistered and cut by rocks and prickly pear cactus spines. Lewis very likely walked the same path as these hikers as he searched for the Great Falls of the Missouri.

35

Day hikers on north bank of the Missouri, near Morony Dam, Great Falls, Montana

36

JUNE 13, 1805

I had proceded on this course about two miles with Goodrich at some distance behind me whin my ears were saluted with the agreeable sound of a fall of water and advancing a little further I saw the spray arrise above the plain like a collumn of smoke . . . which soon began to make a roaring too tremendious to be mistaken for any cause short of the great falls of the Missouri.   here I arrived about 12 OClock having traveled by estimate about 15 Miles. I hurryed down the hill which was about 200 feet high . . . to gaze on this sublimely grand specticle. I took my position on the top of some rocks about 20 feet high opposite the center of the falls. . . . immediately at the cascade the river is about 300 yds. wide; about ninty or a hundred yards of this next the Lard. bluff is a smoth even sheet of water falling over a precipice of at least eighty feet, the remaining part of about 200 yards on my right formes the grandest sight I ever beheld, the hight of the fall is the same of the other but the irregular and somewhat projecting rocks below receives the water in it's passage down and brakes it into a perfect white foam which assumes a thousand forms in a moment sometimes flying up in jets of sparkling foam to the hight of fifteen or twenty feet and are scarcely formed before large roling bodies of the same beaten and foaming water is thrown over and conceals them. in short the rocks seem to be most happily fixed to present a sheet of the whitest beaten froath for 200 yards in length and about 80 feet perpendicular. —MERIWETHER LEWIS

Lewis was on foot in advance of the main party, still uncertain whether he was following the correct river. He had been told about the falls of the Missouri and knew that if he found them the expedition was still on course. The photograph was taken from the same rock Lewis stood on when he first saw the Great Falls, and around the same time in June, when the waters flow over the falls at maximum strength.

37

JUNE 13, 1805

*after wrighting this imperfect discription I again
viewed the falls and was so much disgusted with the
imperfect idea which it conveyed of the scene that I
determined to draw my pen across it and begin agin,
but then reflected that I could not perhaps succeed
better than pening the first impressions of the mind; I
wished for the pencil of Salvator Rosa . . . or the pen
of Thompson, that I might be enabled to give to the
enlightened world some just idea of this truly mag-
niffecent and sublimely grand object, which has from
the commencement of time been concealed from the
view of civilized man; but this was fruitless and
vain. I most sincerely regreted that I had not brought
a crimee obscura with me by the assistance of which
even I could have hoped to have done better but alas
this was also out of my reach; I therefore with the
assistance of my pen only indeavoured to trace some of
the stronger features of this seen . . . and my recollec-
tion aided by some able pencil I hope still to give to
the world some faint idea of an object which at this
moment fills me with such pleasure and astonishment,
and which of it's kind I will venture to ascert is second to but one in the known world.*

—MERIWETHER LEWIS

Ryan Dam surrounds the first of five falls near the city
of Great Falls. The dam was originally built for irriga-
tion purposes but later converted to a hydroelectric
power plant. The water pressure needed to generate
electricity has been compromised by huge silt deposits
in the river and in recent years drought also has pro-
foundly reduced stream flows. What was "a roaring too
tremendious to be mistaken for any cause short of the
great falls of the Missouri," has been silenced for most
days, as the current corporate owners regulate the
drought-diminished water resources and generate electricity for sale to the highest bidder. Modern manage-
ment of the falls means that the "roaring" of waters
over Ryan Dam is most often stopped. Nowadays, the
waters are allowed to spill over the great granite rock
formations for only a couple of weekends in the height
of the summer tourist season. In this photograph, made
in late September when almost no water flows over the
falls, power lines have cast black shadows on Sentinel
Rock.

37

I reached the camp found the Indian woman extreemly ill and much reduced by her indisposition. this gave me some concern as well for the poor object herself, then with a young child in her arms, as from the consideration of her being our only dependence for a friendly negociation with the Snake Indians on whom we depend for horses to assist us in our portage from the Missouri to the columbia River. . . . to procure the water of the Sulpher spring, the virtues of which I now resolved to try on the Indian woman. . . . the water is as transparent as possible strongly impregnated with sulpher, and I suspect Iron also, as the colour of the hills and bluffs in the neighbourhood indicate the existence of that metal. the water to all appearance is precisely similar to that of Bowyer's Sulpher spring in Virginia. . . . I caused her to drink the mineral water altogether. wen I first came down I found that her pulse were scarcely perceptible, very quick frequently irregular and attended with strong nervous symptoms, that of the twitching of the fingers and leaders of the arm; now the pulse had become regular much fuller and a gentle perspiration had taken place

the Indian woman was much better this morning she walked out and gathered a considerable quantity of the white apples of which she eat so heartily in their raw state, together with a considerable quantity of dryed fish without my knowledge that she complained very much and her fever again returned. I rebuked Sharbono severely for suffering her to indulge herself with such food he being privy to it and having been previously told what she must only eat. I now gave her broken dozes of diluted nitre untill it produced perspiration and at 10 P. M. 30 drops of laudnum which gave her a tolerable nights rest.

—MERIWETHER LEWIS

Lewis and Clark often commented about sicknesses suffered by various members of the expedition. Near Great Falls it was Sacagawea's turn to fall ill. Making use of the waters from the sulphur spring, in combination with "two dozes of barks and opium," Lewis tried a new medical treatment. There's been some debate as to the real source of Sacagawea's recovery, but Lewis's use of the spring's water may have helped cure her of a bacterial infection.

38

sulphur springs,
cascade county,
montana

39

portage reenactment,
willow run campsite,
near great falls,
montana

JUNE 22, 1805

This morning early Capt Clark and myself with all the party except Sergt. Ordway Sharbono, Goodrich, york and the Indian woman, set out to pass the portage with the canoe and baggage to the Whitebear Islands, where we intend that this portage shall end. Capt. Clarke piloted us through the plains. about noon we reached a little stream about 8 miles on the portage where we halted and dined; we were obliged here to renew both axeltrees and the tongues and howns of one set of wheels which took us no more than 2 hours. these parts of our carriage had been made of cottonwood and one axetree of an old mast, all of which proved deficient and had broken down several times before we reached this place   we have now renewed them with the sweet willow and hope that they will answer better. after dark we had reached within half a mile of our intended camp when the tongues gave way and we were obliged to leave the canoe, each man took as much of the baggage as he could carry on his back and proceeded to the river where we formed our encampment much fortiegued. the prickly pears were extreemly troublesome to us sticking our feet through our mockersons.

—MERIWETHER LEWIS

At Willow Run, Lewis and Clark found the trees needed to build axles, and the men made cart wheels from cross sections of the cottonwoods and axles (which broke repeatedly) from willow tree trunks. On their arduous overland journey, the Corps hauled enormously heavy dugout canoes and baggage eighteen miles around the present-day city of Great Falls. The portage took one month to complete. On occasion the burden was lessened by powerful northern prairie winds that would catch in the crudely constructed sails mounted on the carts and help push them along.

MAY 11, 1805

I must confess that I do not like the gentlemen and had reather fight two Indians than one bear

MAY 14, 1805

In the evening the men in two of the rear canoes discovered a large brown bear lying in the open grounds about 300 paces from the river, and six of them went out to attack him, all good hunters; they took the advantage of a small eminence which concealed them and got within 40 paces of him unperceived, two of them reserved their fires as had been previously conscerted, the four others fired nearly at the same time and put each his bullet through him, two of the balls passed through the bulk of both lobes of his lungs, in an instant this monster ran at them with open mouth, the two who had reserved their fires discharged their pieces at him as he came towards them, boath of them struck him, one only slightly and the other fortunately broke his shoulder, this however only retarded his motion for a moment only, the men unable to reload their guns took to flight, the bear pursued and had very nearly overtaken them before they reached the river; two of the party betook themselves to a canoe and the others seperated an concealed themselves among the willows, reloaded their pieces, each discharged his piece at him as they had an opportunity they struck him several times again but

the guns served only to direct the bear to them, in this manner he pursued two of them seperately so close that they were obliged to throw aside their guns and pouches and throw themselves into the river altho' the bank was nearly twenty feet perpendicular; so enraged was this anamal that he plunged into the river only a few feet behind the second man he had compelled take refuge in the water, when one of those who still remained on shore shot him through the head and finally killed him; they then took him on shore and butched him when they found eight balls had passed through him in different directions

JUNE 13, 1805

I am induced to believe that the Brown, the white and the Grizly bear of this country are the same species only differing in colour from age or probably from the same natural cause that many other anamals of the same family differ in colour.

—MERIWETHER LEWIS

The men faced several near-fatal encounters with grizzly, or "white," bears, which were unknown in the eastern States. Armed with the latest military rifles, they shot confidently at these ferocious animals, believing them no more invincible to the ball than were the powerful buffalo.

40

fresh bear kill at reenactment camp, near Great Falls, Montana

39

41

thunderstorm over central Montana

JUNE 29, 1805

I perceived a Cloud which appeared black and threaten imediate rain, I looked out for a Shelter but Could See no place without being in great danger of being blown into the river if the wind Should prove as turbelant as it is at Some times. . . . Soon after a torrent of rain and hail fell more violent than ever I Saw before, the rain fell like one voley of water falling from the heavens and gave us time only to get out of the way of a torrent of water which was Poreing down the hill in the rivin with emence force tareing every thing before it takeing with it large rocks & mud, I took my gun & Shot pouch in my left hand, and with the right Scrambled up the hill pushing the Interpreters wife (who had her Child in her arms) before me, the Interpreter himself making attempts to pull up his wife by the hand much Scared and nearly without motion — we at length retched the top of the hill Safe where I found my Servent in Serch of us greatly agitated, for our wellfar—. before I got out of the bottom of the revein which was a flat dry rock when I entered it, the water was up to my waste & wet my watch, I Scrcely got out before it raised 10 feet deep with a torrent which turrouble to behold, and by the time I reached the top of the hill, at least 15 feet water, I directed the party to return to the Camp at the run as fast as possible to get to our lode where Clothes Could be got to Cover the Child whose Clothes were all lost, and the woman who was but just recovering from a Severe indispostion, and was wet and Cold . . . —WILLIAM CLARK

While traveling on the northern Plains, the expedition was subjected to extraordinarily powerful storms. On one occasion, the entire party was caught out in open country and pounded by hailstones seven inches in diameter.

42

on clark's road, looking west, great falls, montana

JUNE 23, 1805

a Cloudy morning wind from the S. E, . . . we eate brackfast of the remaining meat found in Camp & I with the party the truck wheels & poles to Stick up in the prarie as a guide, Set out on our return, we proceeded on, & measured the Way which I Streightened considerably from that I went on yesterday, and arrived at our lower camp . . . found all Safe at Camp   the men mended their mockersons with double Soles to Save their feet from the prickley pear, (which abounds in the Praries,) and the hard ground which in Some & maney places So hard as to hurt the feet verry much . . .
—WILLIAM CLARK

Clark carefully marked the portage route around the five falls by pounding wooden stakes into the ground. He was the mapmaker for the expedition and transcribed the road on his maps. Today it is still possible to follow Clark's exact route. Maps of the portage road can be readily obtained. Climbing from the river to the plains, the route did what most primitive roads do—it followed a ridge line. Here the route goes through the power station and out to the center of the distant trees at the far right.

JULY 1, 1805

the bear were about our camp all last night, we have therefore determined to beat up their quarters tomorrow, and kill them or drive them from their haunts about this place. —MERIWETHER LEWIS

The grizzlies were very aggressive — one brazenly chased a man within 120 feet of the camp before it stopped and turned away. Because of the danger, the captains decided not to let the men go out alone. Lewis theorized that the bears were unusually territorial near the falls because there were many dead buffalo in the water. When the buffalo stopped to drink from the river above the falls, those in front were pushed farther into the water by those in the rear and were then swept over the falls to their death. These buffalo provided an easy source of food for the bears, and they were protecting their food supply. The portage route passes through this cemetery and ends at White Bear Island, so named for its population of grizzly bears.

43

highland cemetery
on clark's road,
great falls, montana

44

gibson park,
great falls, montana

I now began to reflect on this novil occurrence and indeavoured to account for this sudden retreat of the bear. I at first thought that perhaps he had not smelt me before he arrived at the waters edge so near me, but I then reflected that he had pursued me for about 80 or 90 yards before I took the water and on examination saw the grownd toarn with his tallons immediately on the impression of my steps; and the cause of his allarm still remains with me misterious and unaccountable.— so it was and I feelt myself not a little gratifyed that he had declined the combat.

—MERIWETHER LEWIS

Lewis had just shot a buffalo and failed to reload his rifle, not noticing that a full-size grizzly was approaching. The bear charged, and Lewis ran into the water, spinning around to point his espontoon. The grizzly unexpectedly skidded to a halt and ran off, looking over its shoulder as if expecting Lewis to pursue. As an officer Lewis had the privilege of carrying an espontoon as a symbol of his military authority, and at times he used it for a spear, as in this confrontation. This incident occurred in what is today Gibson Park in Great Falls.

45

JUNE 21, 1805

I readily preceive several difficulties in preparing the leather boat which are the want of convenient and proper timber; bark, skins, and above all that of pitch to pay her seams, a deficiency that I really know not how to surmount unless it be by means of tallow and pounded charcoal which mixture has answered a very good purpose on our wooden canoes heretofore.

JUNE 24, 1805

on my arrival at the upper camp this morning, I found that Sergt. Gass and Shields had made but slow progress in collecting timber for the boat; they complained of great difficulty in geting streight or even tolerably streight sticks of 4½ feet long. we were obliged to make use of the willow and box alder, the cottonwood being too soft and brittle.

JULY 5, 1805

This morning I had the boat removed to an open situation. . . . I then set a couple of men to pounding of charcoal to form a composition with some beeswax which we have and buffaloe tallow now my only hope and resource for paying my boat; I sincerely hope it may answer yet I fear it will not.

JULY 9, 1805

we discovered that a greater part of the composition had seperated from the skins and left the seams of the boat exposed to the water and she leaked in such manner that she would not answer. I need not add that this circumstance mortifyed me not a little; and to prevent her leaking without pich was impossible with us, and to obtain this article was equally impossible, therefore the evil was irraparable. . . . I therefore relinquished all further hope of my favorite boat and ordered her to be sunk in the water, that the skins might become soft in order the better to take her in peices tomorrow and deposite the iron fraim at this place as it could probably be of no further service to us.

—MERIWETHER LEWIS

Thomas Jefferson believed that Lewis and Clark would find a passage over the mountains, which, when crossed, would lead to down-coursing rivers flowing toward the Pacific Ocean. The President speculated that there might even be a lake at the summit whose waters drained in both east and west directions. Lewis and Clark, too, expected only a short portage would be necessary to complete the Northwest Passage. Guided by this notion while he was in Harpers Ferry overseeing building of their boat, Lewis had designed an iron-framed boat as an experiment, estimating that it would carry 1,700 pounds. Up until this point in their journey, the men had carried the heavy pieces of his experiment. They assembled the boat after completing the portage around the falls, but there were no pine trees with which to make pitch to seal its seams. After trying in vain to make the boat sound, they abandoned it. Today, researchers continue to hunt for the boat's frame.

Drewyer killed a buffaloe this morning near the river and we halted and breakfasted on it. here for the first time I ate of the small guts of the buffaloe cooked . . . over a blazing fire in the Indian stile without any preperation of washing or other clensing and found them very good. —*After breakfast I determined to leave Capt. C. and party, and go on to the point where the river enters the Rocky Mountains and make the necessary observations against their arrival; accordingly I set out with the two invalleds Potts and LaPage and Drewyer*

—MERIWETHER LEWIS

Before the Plains Indians rode horses, they hunted buffalo on foot. One method they used was to trigger a stampede and chase the buffalo over a cliff. These cliff edges became known as buffalo jumps. In Lewis's account of how this was done, after the Indians had surrounded a herd, a young hunter disguised as a buffalo would run ahead and lead the buffalo over the cliff— "the disguised indian or decoy has taken care to place himself sufficiently nigh the buffalo to be noticed by them when they take to flight and runing before them they follow him in full speede to the precipice. . . ." If the animals survived the fall, they were so badly injured that the Indians could finish them off easily with stone weapons. Overkills were common with this method, and along the upper Missouri the captains noted several jumps, identifiable by hundreds of bison bones. The expedition was in the river on the left side of this view. Square Butte, which Lewis named Fort Mountain, can be seen in the distance.

46

ulm pishkin buffalo jump and table mountain, montana

JULY 4, 1805

Capt. C. completed a draught of the river from Fort Mandan to this place which we intend depositing at this place in order to guard against accedents. not having seen the Snake Indians or knowing in fact whether to calculate on their friendship or hostility or friendship we have conceived our party sufficiently small and therefore have concluded not to dispatch a canoe with a part of our men to St. Louis as we had intended early in the spring. we fear also that such a measure might possibly discourage those who would in such case remain, and might possibly hazzard the fate of the expedition. we have never once hinted to any one of the party that we had such a scheme in contemplation, and all appear perfectly to have made up their minds to suceed in the expedition or purish in the attempt. we all beleive that we are now about to enter on the most perilous and difficult part of our voyage, yet I see no one repining; all appear ready to met those difficulties which wait us with resolution and becoming fortitude. . . . the Mountains to the N. W. & W. of us are still entirely covered are white and glitter with the reflection of the sun.

—MERIWETHER LEWIS

With the failure of the iron boat, the men needed to make two dugout canoes large enough to carry their baggage. Lewis doubted that they'd find cottonwood trees of adequate size, but luckily they located two trees with twenty-five and thirty-three feet of usable length. After five days of carving and thirty miles of upstream travel from Great Falls, they entered the Rocky Mountains. They camped at the base of the distant, tall, rocky peak in the photograph, which is now called Eagle Rock. Clark led a party ashore in hopes of discovering Shoshone Indians. They had not seen a single Indian since leaving Fort Mandan, some eight hundred miles back. Because gunfire from hunting might frighten away the Indians, Lewis thought Clark's party should go in advance to tell the Indians of the expedition's friendly intentions. Guns could mean that the Shoshone's enemies, the Blackfeet, were on the river. The Blackfeet were the best-armed Indians on the northern Plains.

48

Missouri River, near
cascade, Montana

JULY 15, 1805

*We arrose very early this morning, assigned the canoes
their loads and had it put on board. we now found
our vessels eight in number all heavily laden, notwith-
standing our several deposits; tho' it is true we have
now a considerable stock of dryed meat and grease. we
find it extreemly difficult to keep the baggage of many
of our men within reasonable bounds; they will be
adding bulky articles of but little use or value to them.
At 10 A. M. we once more saw ourselves fairly under
way much to my joy and I beleive that of every individual who compose the party. I walked on shore and
killed 2 Elk near one of which the party halted and
dined.* —MERIWETHER LEWIS

48

49

JULY 20, 1805

The Misquetors verry troublesom   my man York nearly tired out, the bottoms of my feet blistered. I observe a Smoke rise to our right up the Valley of the last Creek about 12 miles distant, The Cause of this Smoke I can't account for certainly tho' think it probable that the Indians have heard the Shooting of the Partey below, and Set the Praries or Valey on fire to allarm their Camps; Supposeing our party to be a war party comeing against them, I left Signs to Shew the Indians if they Should come on our trail that we were not their enemeys. Camped on the river, the feet of the men with me So Stuck with Prickley pear & cut with the Stones that they were Scerseley able to march at a Slow gate this after noon

—WILLIAM CLARK

As the expedition approached Shoshone country, it went through a narrow river passage, and Sacagawea recognized familiar country. So steep and narrow were the river's sides that Lewis worried a waterfall lay ahead, despite her reassurances. Lewis hoisted small flags to signal to the Indians that they were not enemies and put Sacagawea in the front of the lead canoe because women never accompanied warriors. Clark, still on shore, saw signs of Indians but failed to make any contact with them. Today, the twenty-five-mile-long Canyon Ferry Lake fills the area.

49

50

Three forks of the
Missouri, Montana

Both Capt. C. and myself corrisponded in opinon with rispect to the impropriety of calling either of these streams the Missouri and accordingly agreed to name them after the President of the United States and the Secretaries of the Treasury and state having previously named one river in honour of the Secretaries of War and Navy. In pursuance of this resolution we called the S. W. fork, that which we meant to ascend, Jefferson's River in honor of Thomas Jefferson. . . . the Middle fork we called Madison's River in honor of James Madison, and the S. E. Fork we called Gallitin's River in honor of Albert Gallitin. . . . Our present camp is precisely on the spot that the Snake Indians were encamped at the time the Minnetares of the Knife R. first came in sight of them five years since. . . . the Minnetares pursued, attacked them, killed 4 men 4 women a number of boys, and mad prisoners of all the females and four boys, Sah-cah-gar-we-ah or Indian woman was one of the female prisoners taken at that time; tho' I cannot discover that she shews any immotion of sorrow in recollecting this event, or of joy in being again restored to her native country; if she has enough to eat and a few trinkets to wear I beleive she would be perfectly content anywhere. —MERIWETHER LEWIS

The photograph was taken from the same rocky overlook where Lewis stood when he observed the junction of the three rivers and named them. The expedition camped here, at the same place Sacagawea was captured, and spent time trying to determine which fork to follow to reach the Continental Divide.

the Indian woman recognized the point of a high plain to our right which she informed us was not very distant from the summer retreat of her nation on a river beyond the mountains which runs to the west. this hill she says her nation calls the beaver's head from a conceived remblance of it's figure to the head of that animal. she assures us that we shall either find her people on this river or on the river immediately west of it's source; which from it's present size cannot be very distant. as it is now all important with us to meet with those people as soon as possible, I deter-mined . . . to proceed tomorrow with a small party . . . untill I found the Indians; in short it is my reso-lusion to find them or some others, who have horses if it should cause me a trip of one month. for without horses we shall be obliged to leave a great part of our stores, of which, it appears to me that we have a stock already sufficiently small for the length of the voyage before us. —MERIWETHER LEWIS

As the expedition moved along the river, it became increasingly difficult to pull the boats upstream in the shallow water, and they desperately wanted to trade for horses. Though the Corps was in Shoshone Indian country, they had gone almost nine hundred miles without seeing an Indian.

51

Beaverhead Rock
and River, near
Dillon, Montana

52

AUGUST 11, 1805

*whe[n] I arrived within about 150 paces I again
repepeated the word tab-ba-bone and held up the
trinkits in my hands and striped up my shirt sleve to
give him an opportunity of seeing the colour of my
skin and advanced leasure towards him but he did
not remain untill I got nearer than about 100 paces
when he suddonly turned his hose about, gave him
the whip leaped the creek and disapeared in the willow brush in an instant and with him vanished all
my hopes of obtaining horses for the preasent. I now
felt quite as much mortification and disappointment
as I had pleasure and expectation at the first sight of
this indian. I fet soarly chargrined at the conduct of
the men particularly Sheilds to whom I principally
attributed this failure in obtaining an introduction to
the natives. I now called the men to me and could not
forbare abraiding them a little for their want of
attention and imprudence on this occasion.*

—MERIWETHER LEWIS

The Beaverhead River had turned into a small trout
stream, hardly deep enough to float the canoes. The
Continental Divide was just a few miles away, and it
was critical for the expedition to make contact with the
Shoshone and secure horses. Lewis and three men had
formed an advance party and were following an Indian
trail that led toward the pass when they finally spied an
Indian on horseback. Lewis and the men were walking
spread out, and the men did not hear Lewis's order to
halt. He threw a blanket into the air and then onto the
ground, signaling a desire for a parley, but the Indian
was suspicious because the other men, who were carrying rifles, continued to advance. Historians speculate
that in calling out "Tab-ba-bone" Lewis may have
thought he was saying "Ti-yo-bo-nin," which means
"I'm a white man!" Instead, his cries may have been
meaningless, or very possibly they could have sounded
threatening.

This day I completed my thirty first year, and conceived that I had in all human probability now existed about half the period which I am to remain in this Sub-lunary world. I reflected that I had as yet done but little, very little indeed, to further the hapiness of the human race, or to advance the information of the succeeding generation. I viewed with regret the many hours I have spent in indolence, and now soarly feel the want of that information which those hours would have given me had they been judiciously expended. but since they are past and cannot be recalled, I dash from me the gloomy thought and resolved in future, to redouble my exertions and at least indeavour to promote those two primary objects of human existence, by giving them the aid of that portion of talents which nature and fortune have bestoed on me; or in future, to live for <u>mankind</u>, as I have heretofore lived <u>for myself</u>.

——MERIWETHER LEWIS

Somewhere in the center depths of the reservoir lies the campsite where Lewis and Clark prepared to ascend the mountains and pass through the Continental Divide. Here they sunk their canoes and secreted their supplies, intending to use them on the return trip. In preparing to haul their baggage over the Pass, the men made many trips between this campsite and the summit of the Beaverhead Mountains, which appear in the background. Four years after this birthday Lewis would commit suicide.

53

site of camp fortunate,
clark canyon reservoir,
montana

54

Where Lewis thought the Missouri River began

AUGUST 12, 1805

the road took us to the most distant fountain of the waters of the mighty Missouri in surch of which we have spent so many toilsome days and wristless nights. thus far I had accomplished one of those great objects on which my mind has been unalterably fixed for many years, judge then of the pleasure I felt in allying my thirst with this pure and ice cold water which issues from the base of a low mountain. . . . two miles below McNeal had exultingly stood with a foot on each side of this little rivulet and thanked his god that he had lived to bestride the mighty & heretofore deemed endless Missouri. —MERIWETHER LEWIS

Shortly after they had crossed Lemhi Pass, the expedition encounterd the Shoshone Indians. In a miraculous coincidence, Sacagawea recognized her brother Cameahwait, who was their chief, at once clinching the successful outcome of their horse-trading. Lewis mistakenly thought that they had reached the source of the Missouri, but the river's source is at the head of Red Rock River. This man stands with his feet astride a water pipe at the place where Lewis thought the river began.

55

AUGUST 12, 1805

after refreshing ourselves we proceeded on to the top of the dividing ridge from which I discovered immence ranges of high mountains still to the West of us with their tops partially covered with snow. I now decended the mountain about ¾ of a mile . . . to a handsome bold running Creek of cold Clear water. here I first tasted the water of the great Columbia river.
—MERIWETHER LEWIS

This photograph looks west from the Continental Divide toward the endless expanse of the Bitterroot Mountain range. Lewis saw a similar view at Lemhi Pass, which ended any hope for a northwest passage by water to the Pacific. Lewis and Clark Pass is 6,284 feet in elevation, and was used by Lewis on the return trip as a shortcut between present-day Missoula and Great Falls, Montana. Lewis's route followed well-used Indian trails that led up Alice Creek to the summit, which was shaped like a saddle. Today jeeps and hikers take the same route in coming up from the distant valley. The approach to the pass still shows scars left on the land by the Nez Perce's travois, the poles dragging and cutting into the bare earth, as they drove their horses through the Divide and over the mountains to trade with the Plains Indians.

I can discover that these people are by no means friendly to the Spaniard their complaint is, that the Spaniards will not let them have fire arms and amunition, that they put them off by telling them that if they suffer them to have guns they will kill each other, thus leaving them defenceless and an easy prey to their bloodthirsty neighbours to the East of them, who being in possession of fire arms hunt them up and murder them without rispect to sex or age and plunder them of their horses on all occasions. they told me that to avoid their enemies who were eternally harrassing them that they were obliged to remain in the interior of these mountains at least two thirds of the year where the[y] suffered as we then saw great heardships for the want of food sometimes living for weeks without meat and only a little fish roots and berries. but this added Cameahwait, with his ferce eyes and lank jaws grown meager for the want of food, would not be the case if we had guns. . . . I told them that . . . after our finally returning to our homes towards the rising sun whitemen would come to them with an abundance of guns and every other article necessary to their defence and comfort, and that they would be enabled to supply themselves with these articles on reasonable terms in exchange for the skins of the

beaver Otter and Ermin so abundant in their country. they expressed great pleasure at this information and said they had been long anxious to see the whitemen that traded guns; and that we might rest assured of their friendship and that they would do whatever we wished them. —MERIWETHER LEWIS

At last, the expedition was on horseback. They had succeeded in moving their supplies over the Lemhi Pass and were traveling north toward the Bitterroot Valley, led by their Shoshone guide whom they named "Old Toby." Along the way they encountered the Salish Indians, allies of the Shoshone, and they bartered for more animals, giving them a total of thirty-nine horses, three colts, and a mule. The Salish traded some of their five hundred horses for steel battle axes and knives. Trade with Chief Cameahwait required a different strategy—the promise that the Americans would return from St. Louis and bring guns for the Shoshone.

56

Bitterroot Mountains, near Conner, Montana

55

58

57

AUGUST 23, 1805

*Capt. C. halted here about 2 hours, caught some
small fish, on which, with the addition of some
berries, they dined. the river . . . was one continued
rapid, in which there were five shoals neither of
which could be passed with loaded canoes nor even
run with empty ones. at those several places therefore
it would be necessary to unload and transport the
baggage for a considerable distance over steep and
almost inacassable rocks where there was no possibility
of employing horses for the releif of the men; the
canoes would next have to be let down by cords*

—MERIWETHER LEWIS

The Salmon headed due west through the mountains,
and Lewis and Clark thought it would eventually connect with other rivers that emptied into the Columbia,
which was known to be the only river in the northern
reaches that flowed into the Pacific Ocean. The Indians
had warned them that the Salmon was impassable, but
Clark followed the river, hoping it would provide a way
west and allow them to abandon their horses for canoes,
but he discovered his error. This is where he determined
the river could not be navigated.

SEPTEMBER 5, 1805

these Savages has the Strangest language of any we have ever Seen. they appear to us to have an Empeddiment in their Speech or a brogue or bur on their tongue but they are the likelyest and honestst Savages we have ever yet Seen. . . . we all suppose these Indians to be the Welch nation of Indians, if there be any such a Nation; & from their language we believe them to be the same. Captain Lewis took down the names of almost every thing in their language in order to find whether they are the same

—JOSEPH WHITEHOUSE

As the expedition traveled along the edge of the impenetrable Bitterroot Mountains and down the valley where present-day Hamilton lies, they encountered a strange-speaking tribe that Private Whitehouse identified as "Welch Indians." A myth dating back to 1583 told the story of a Welsh prince named Madoc who had discovered America in 1170 A.D. He was supposed to have gone back to Wales, gathered a group of colonists, and returned to the New World, only to disappear in the western wilderness. The lost colonists were believed to have intermarried with the Indians, and to still speak a version of the Welsh language. Jefferson's instructions had included looking out for this tribe, as well as for any mountains of salt or any live mastodons.

Before they found the Lolo Trail, which would provide an opening to the West, the expedition had marched two hundred miles north from Lemhi Pass. This is almost the same distance they had traveled following the Missouri River south to the Continental Divide. On the return trip, they took a shortcut of about fifty miles across the mountains, saving themselves four hundred miles. While the Bitterroot Valley had a river, the captains surmised from the absence of salmon that they would encounter a large falls downstream and decided, correctly, that it was premature to return to the river.

58

Ravalli County Fair, Hamilton, Montana

59

Lolo Trail begins about ten miles south of Missoula, Montana, and heads west up Lolo Creek into the Bitterroot Mountains where it encounters a dizzying series of ridges going in a westerly direction. On the trail the Corps experienced both luck and disappointment. They came upon a Nez Perce Indian who was crossing from the other side, and he agreed to guide them. But, first, the men needed to find their stray horses; perhaps bored by the delay, the Indian decided not to wait and left. They now found themselves with neither game to hunt nor grass for their horses to eat. Without food and near to perishing, the party split up, sending Clark and a small party of hunters ahead to find help. It took eleven days, covering 160 miles, for the men to cross the Bitterroots in one of America's truly heroic marches. This pile of rocks, known as the Indian Post Office, lies near the high point of the Lolo Trail. There is no good explanation for the name of the rock pile, which has changed in height over the years.

59

indian post office on Lolo Trail, Bitterroot Mountains, Idaho

60

Bathers at Killed Colt
Creek, Bitterroot
Mountains, Idaho

SEPTEMBER 14, 1805

a Cloudy day in the Valies it rained and hailed, on the top of the mountains Some Snow fell   we Set out early . . . and Crossd a verry high Steep mountain. . . . I could see no fish, and the grass entirely eaten out by the horses, we proceeded on 2 miles & Encamped opposit a Small Island at the mouth of a branch on the right side of the river which is at this place 80 yards wide, Swift and Stoney, here we wer compelled to kill a Colt for our men & Selves to eat for the want of meat & we named the South fork Colt killed Creek, and this river we Call <u>Flathead</u> *River — . . . The flat head name is Koos koos ke R.* —WILLIAM CLARK

Lewis doubted his Shoshone guide's knowledge of the route, and he was right. Old Toby promptly got lost and led them off the ridge, downhill some one thousand feet, to the Kooskooskee River, which proved a dead end. The men had to turn around and with difficulty go back up the mountain.

60

61

SEPTEMBER 15, 1805

Several horses Sliped and roled down Steep hills which hurt them verry much   The one which Carried my desk & Small trunk Turned over & roled down a mountain for 40 yards & lodged against a tree, broke the Desk the horse escaped and appeared but little hurt. . . . after two hours delay we proceeded on up the mountain Steep & ruged as usial, more timber near the top, when we arrived at the top As we Conceved we could find no water and Concluded to Camp and make use of the Snow we found on the top to cook the remnt. of our Colt & make our Supe, evening verry Cold and Cloudy. Two of our horses gave out, pore and too much hurt to proceed on and left in the rear — nothing killed to day except 2 Phests.

From this mountain I could observe high ruged mountains in every direction as far as I could See.

—WILLIAM CLARK

While Clark's advance party struggled along the Lolo Trail, Lewis reported that Sergeant Frazier's horse fell from a nearly perpendicular cliff, dropping three hundred feet, but it was not injured in what Lewis described as the "most wonderfull escape I ever witnessed." Forest Road 500 follows closely and is sometimes even directly on top of the trail. By mid-September the snowfall usually begins, making the mountains impassable until June. Today's map of the road contains names given by the captains, reflecting their struggle: Snow Camp, Bears Oil and Roots, Hungry Creek Camp, Portable Soup Camp, and Horse Sweat Pass.

SEPTEMBER 16, 1805

began to Snow about 3 hours before Day and Continud all day   the Snow in The morning 4 Inches deep on The old Snow, and by night we found it from 6 to 8 Inches deep   I walked in front to keep the road and found great dificuelty in keeping it as in maney places the Snow had entirely filled up the track. . . . I have been wet and as cold in every part as I ever was in my life, indeed I was at one time fearfull my feet would freeze in the thin mockersons which I wore

—WILLIAM CLARK

After Lewis's party killed their last colt for food, their situation was desperate. Two days later, they came upon a freshly killed horse that Clark's advance party had left on the trail for Lewis and the other men. With it was a note saying that he was proceeding over the Bitterroots to the prairies to hunt for more food. The next day Lewis met one of Clark's men coming back; he brought dried fish and roots that Clark had obtained from friendly contact with the Nez Perce Indians.

62

Footprints on the Lolo Trail, Bitterroot Mountains, Idaho

63

SEPTEMBER 25, 1805

when I arrived at Camp found Capt Lewis verry Sick, Several men also verry Sick, I gave Some Salts & Tarter emetic, we deturmined to go to where the best timbr was and there form a Camp

SEPTEMBER 27, 1805

all the men able to work comened building 5 Canoes, Several taken Sick at work, our hunters returned Sick without meet. J. Colter returned he found only one of the lost horses, on his way killed a deer, half of which he gave the Indians the other proved nourishing to the Sick   The day verry hot, we purchase fresh Salmon of them   Several Indians Come up the river from a Camp Some distance below   Capt Lewis very Sick nearly all the men Sick. our Shoshonee Indian Guide employed himself makeing flint points for his arrows

OCTOBER 7, 1805

I continu verry unwell but obliged to attend every thing   all the Canoes put into the water and loaded, fixed our Canoes as well as possible and Set out   as we were about to Set out we missd. both of the Chiefs who promised to accompany us; I also missed my Pipe Tomahawk which Could not be found.

The after part of the day Cloudy proceeded on passed lo rapids which wer danjerous   the Canoe in which I was Struck a rock and Sprung a leak in the 3rd rapid

— WILLIAM CLARK

After clearing the Bitterroot Mountains, the expedition arrived in Nez Perce Indian country. Tribal legend has it that they planned to kill the white men, which would have been an easy job since they were all sick with dysentery from gorging on dried salmon and camas roots. The Indians were dissuaded from this action by one of their women who had been captured by the Blackfeet and sold into slavery in Canada where the white people had treated her fairly. Had the Nez Perce carried out their plan they would have been the best-armed tribe west of the Rockies as well as the richest in trade goods. Instead, Chief Twisted Hair fed the expedition in exchange for goods, drew them a map to the Clearwater River and beyond, and led them to a spot near these road signs where trees large enough to make canoes were growing. The men manufactured five canoes in ten days despite the fact that nearly all of them were sick the entire time. Most helpful was Clark's decision to implement the Indian method of burning out the centers of the logs, instead of chopping them laboriously by hand. Chief Twisted Hair also promised to look after the horses until their return.

63

OCTOBER 16, 1805

*after we had our camp fixed and fires made, a Chief
came from their Camp which was about ¼ of a mile
up the Columbia river at the head of about 200 men
Singing and beeting on their drums Stick and keeping
time to the musik, they formed a half circle around us
and Sung for Some time, we gave them all Smoke,
and Spoke to their Chiefs as well as we could by Signs
informing them of our friendly disposition to all
nations, and our joy in Seeing those of our Children
around us, Gave the principal chief a large Medal
Shirt and Handkf. a 2 nd Chief a Meadel of Small
Size, and to the Cheif who came down from the
upper villages a Small <u>medal</u> & Handkerchief.*

OCTOBER 18, 1805

*The Great Chief and one of the <u>Chim-Nâ Pum</u>
nation . . . drew me a Sketch of the Columbia above
and the tribes of his nation, living on the bank, and
its waters.*

*We thought it necessary to lay in a Store of
Provisions for our voyage, and the fish being out
of Season, we purchased forty dogs for which we
gave articles of little value, Such as bells, thimbles,
knitting pins, brass wire & a few beeds all of which
they appeared well Satisfied and pleased.*

*every thing being arranged we took in our Two
Chiefs, and Set out on the great Columbia river*
—WILLIAM CLARK

The Clearwater River connects to the Snake, which in
turn joins the Columbia near present-day Kenniwick,
Washington. The Columbia seemed to hold the promise of a swift downriver journey of about three hundred
miles to the Pacific, but the captains discovered that the
river was full of rapids and dangerous falls, and that a
huge Indian population lived along its banks. Today a
number of dams have created enormous lakes, replacing
what was once a fast and treacherous river with mostly
placid water.

64

grain elevators, entrance
to columbia river gorge,
looking west, lake
wallula, oregon

65

OCTOBER 19, 1805

I landed in front of five Lodges . . . Saw no person the enteranc or Dores of the Lodges wer Shut . . . I approached one with a pipe in my hand entered a lodge which was the nearest to me found 32 persons men, women and a few children Setting permiscuesly in the Lodg . . . in the greatest agutation, Some crying and ringing there hands, others hanging their heads. I gave my hand to them all and made Signs of my friendly dispotion and offered the men my pipe to Smok and distributed a fiew Small articles which I had in my pockets,—this measure passified those distressed people verry much, I then Sent one man into each lodge and entered a Second myself the inhabitants of which I found more fritened than those of the first lodge. . . . I then . . . Set my Self on a rock and made Signs to the men to come and Smoke with me. . . . the Indians came out & Set by me and Smoked   They said we came from the clouds . . . and were not men —WILLIAM CLARK

Looming over the Columbia River near the entrance to the gorge, Hat Rock was given its name by the captains. Clark came upon these frightened Umatilla Indians on the river below Hat Rock. He was traveling ahead of Lewis and the main party (who were negotiating the rapids), and so what had been a standard procedure in this section of river—to send ahead their Nez Perce guides, Twisted Hair and Tetoharsky, to tell tribes of their peaceful intentions—had not been followed.

65

66

mount hood and
the dalles, oregon

OCTOBER 19, 1805

I assended a high clift about 200 feet above the water from the top of which is a leavel plain extending up the river and off for a great extent . . . from this place I descovered a high mountain of emence hight covered with Snow, this must be one of the mountains laid down by Vancouver, as Seen from the mouth of the Columbia River . . . I take it to be Mt. St. Helens, destant 156 miles. —WILLIAM CLARK

George Vancouver's maps, which charted 119 upstream miles of the Columbia River, had been drawn thirteen years earlier, but Vancouver, who was a British sea captain, missed discovering the Columbia River. Instead, its discovery was credited to an American, Captain Robert Gray, who named but did not explore the river. Clark was using Vancouver's maps when he identified some peaks with the names that Vancouver had given them. Historians today believe the mountain that Clark saw in the distance was not Mount St. Helens but Mount Adams. The day before the expedition had spotted another distant peak, which they believed to be Mount Hood.

66

OCTOBER 29, 1805

A cloudy morning wind from the West but not hard, we Set out at day light, and proceeded on about five miles   Came too on the Stard. Side at a village of 7 houses built in the Same form and materials of those above. . . . I observed in the lodge of the Chief Sundery articles which must have been precured from the white people, Such a Scarlet & blue Cloth Sword Jacket & hat. I also observed two wide Split boards with images on them Cut and painted in emitation of a man. . . .

The Chief then directed his wife to hand him his medison bag which he opened and Showed us 14 fingers . . . which he Said was the fingers of his ene-mies which he had taken in war . . . this is the first Instance I ever knew of the Indians takeing any other trofea of their exploits off the dead bodies of their Enimies except the Scalp.— The Chief painted those fingers with Several other articles which was in his bag red and Securely put them back, haveing first mad a Short harrang which I Suppose was bragging of what he had done in war. we purchased 12 Dogs and 4 Sacks of fish, & Some fiew ascid berries, after brackfast we proceeded on —WILLIAM CLARK

Their Nez Perce guides warned the captains of a plan they'd overheard to attack the expedition by the Wishrom–Wasco tribes who populated the area. When they reached the mouth of Chenoweth Creek and the Columbia River, the guides were afraid to continue, fearing they would be killed on sight because they were at war with the downriver tribes. The captains built a campsite with defense in mind and chose a high rock that is now a well-marked site in The Dalles, about two miles from the view in this photograph.

This is where the overland journey of the Oregon Trail ended. After 1836, westward settlers would load their wagons on crude and overpriced rafts on the creek to be floated downriver near to what is now Portland, Oregon. In 1845, the Barlow toll road opened, a cheaper alternative, which took pioneers over the shoulder of Mount Hood, providing they crossed before October when the snows began to fall.

67

End of the Oregon Trail, The Dalles, Oregon

69

68

umatilla indian with
salmon net, near
cascade locks, oregon

NOVEMBER 1, 1805

*The nativs of the waters of the Columbia appear
helthy, Some have tumers on different parts of their
bodies, and Sore and weak Eyes are common, maney
have lost their Sight entirely great numbers with one
eye out. . . . maney have worn their teeth down and
Some quite into their gums, this I cannot Satisfactorily
account for it, do ascribe it in some measure to their
method of eateing, their food, roots pertiularly, which
they make use of as they are taken out of the earth frequently nearly covered with Sand. . . . They . . . have
all flat heads in this quarter . . . They are [d]irty in
the extream, both in their person and cooking. . . . I
observed in maney of the villeages which I have
passed, the heads of the female children in the press
for the purpose of compressing their heads in their
infancy into a certain form, between two boards.*
—WILLIAM CLARK

Native Americans living in the Bonneville Dam region
have the legal right to fish for salmon for personal con-
sumption using traditional nets of the type seen here.
From a platform overhanging the river, this Umatilla
Indian can operate his net. He will usually fish near a
small falls where, during their migration, the salmon
swim or jump upriver and into his net.

OCTOBER 31, 1805

one of the men Shot a goose above this Great Shute, which was floating into the Shute when an Indian observed it, plunged into the water & Swam to the Goose and brought in on Shore, at the head of the Suck. . . . as this Indian richly earned the goose I Suffered him to keep it which he about half picked and Spited it up with the guts in it to roste.

This Great Shute or falls is about ½ a mile with the water of this great river Compressed within the Space of 150 paces in which there is great numbers of both large and Small rocks, water passing with great velocity forming & boiling in a most horriable manner, with a fall of about 20 feet, below it widens to about 200 paces and current gentle for a Short distance. —WILLIAM CLARK

Along the Columbia River native people harvested great quantities of salmon. Clark once saw what he estimated to be ten thousand pounds of salmon drying in a village. After the men had suffered severe dysentery from overeating what may have been tainted salmon, they preferred meat, but game was scarce in the Columbia River Gorge, and so they bought dogs from the Indians. Completed in 1938, Bonneville Dam has attracted increasing numbers of sturgeon to the area. The sturgeon now eagerly consume small fish that get caught and chewed into pieces by the dam's turbines. As a result, the spillway has become a principal feeding ground for sturgeon. The fish grow so large that any sturgeon shorter than fifty inches must be thrown back in the river.

69

Man with a sturgeon, Bonneville Dam, Oregon

NOVEMBER 1, 1805

A verry Cool morning wind hard from the N. E. The Indians who arrived last evining took their Canoes on ther Sholders and Carried them below the Great Shute, we Set about takeing our Small Canoe and all the baggage by land 940 yards of bad Slippery and rockey way   The Indians we discoverd took ther loading the whole length of the portage 2 ½ miles, to avoid a Second Shute which appears verry bad to pass, and thro' which they passed with their empty canoes. Great numbers of Sea Otters, they are So cautious that I with dificuelty got a Shot at one to day, which I must have killed, but could not get him as he Sunk

. . . I cannot lern certainly as to the traffick those Inds. carry on below, if white people or the indians who trade with the Whites who are either Settled or visit the mouth of this river. I believe mostly with the latter as their knowledge of the white people appears to be verry imperfect, and the articles which they appear to trade mostly i e' Pounded fish, Beargrass, and roots; cannot be an object of comerce with furin merchants —WILLIAM CLARK

In earlier times the Columbia River descended for about fifty miles through a series of spectacular rapids and falls, several of which would be rated class-five rapids today. Chinook Indians lined the banks by the hundreds to watch the white men's clumsy dugout canoes shoot the rapids, hoping that the explorers would be killed and they could recover their supplies and trade goods. The men of the Corps who knew how to swim ran the canoes while the others portaged baggage around the rapids. At the site of the Cascade Locks, the rapids were so dangerous that everything, including canoes, was portaged around. To enable steamboat traffic up the Columbia, the Great Shute Falls, which presented such tremendous obstacles to Lewis and Clark, were submerged by the lock and dam construction. The canal and locks were completed in 1896. All of what was once wild waterway is under dams. A natural bridge over the river, called the Bridge of the Gods in local Indian legends, was destroyed by a landslide. What was left of the bridge created the series of rapids that slowed the expedition down on this stretch of the Columbia.

70

school group at cascade locks and bridge of the gods, columbia river, oregon

71

OCTOBER 28, 1805

A cool windey morning we loaded our Canoes and Set out at 9 oClock, a. m. . . . at four miles we landed at a village of 8 houses on the Stard. Side. . . . I entered one of the houses in which I Saw a British musket, a cutlash . . . and Several brass Tea kittles of which they appeared verry fond. . . . here we purchased five Small Dogs, Some dried buries, & white bread made of roots, the wind rose and we were obliged to lie by all day. . . . we had not been long on Shore before a Canoe came up with a man woman & 2 children, who had a fiew roots to Sell, Soon after maney others joined them from above, The wind which is the cause of our delay, does not retard the motions of those people at all, as their canoes are calculated to ride the highest waves, they are built of white cedar or Pine verry light wide in the middle and tapers at each end, with aperns, and heads of animals carved on the bow. . . . wind blew hard accompanied with rain all the evening . . . we encamped on the Sand wet and disagreeable one Deer killed this evening, and another wounded near our Camp. —WILLIAM CLARK

The Corps' bulky dugout canoes proved inadequate against the powerful winds in the Columbia River Gorge, which today are a major attraction for wind surfers. The strong winds result when cold ocean air is funneled through the high canyon walls toward the hot interior of eastern Washington; by midday in summer, they easily reach a steady thirty miles an hour.

72

NOVEMBER 4, 1805
*Several Canoes of Indians from the village above
came down . . . Those fellows we found assumeing
and disagreeable. . . .*

*dureing the time we were at dinner those fellows
Stold my pipe Tomahawk which They were Smoking
with, I imediately Serched every man and the canoes,
but Could find nothing of my Tomahawk, while
Serching for the Tomahawk one of those Scoundals
Stole a Cappoe [great coat] . . . which was found
Stufed under the root of a treer, near the place they
Sat*

NOVEMBER 5, 1805
*Rained all the after part of last night, rain continues
this morning, I [s]lept but verry little last night for
the noise Kept dureing the whole of the night by the
Swans, Geese, white & Grey Brant Ducks &c. on a
Small Sand Island close under the Lard. Side; they
were emensely noumerous, and their noise horid. . . .
This is the first night which we have been entirely
clear of Indians Since our arrival on the waters of
the Columbia River. We made 32 miles to day by
estimation —*

NOVEMBER 7, 1805
*Great joy in camp we are in <u>view</u> of the <u>ocian</u>, . . .
this great Pacific Octean which we been So long anxious to See. and the roreing or noise made by the
waves brakeing on the rockey Shores (as I Suppose)
may be heard distictly*
—WILLIAM CLARK

As the men drew closer to the Pacific Ocean, they could
feel and see the tidal effects of the great body of water
ahead of them. The Trojan nuclear plant, which began
operating in 1976, was closed in 1992 because of safety-
system failures. In 1999, its reactor parts were shipped
upriver to the Hanford Nuclear Reservation storage
facility in Richland, Washington, but its spent nuclear
fuel rods remain here, embedded in concrete.

A Tremendious wind from the S. W. about 3 oClock
this morning with Lightineng and hard claps of
Thunder, and Hail which Continued untill 6 oClock
a. m. when it became light for a Short time, then the
heavens became Sudenly darkened by a black Cloud
from the S. W. and rained with great violence untill
12 oClock, the waves tremendious brakeing with
great fury against the rocks and trees on which we
were encamped. our Situation is dangerous. we took
the advantage of a low <u>tide</u> and moved our camp
around a point to a Small wet bottom at the mouth
of a Brook, which we had not observed when we
Came to this cove; from it being verry thick and
obscured by drift trees and thick bushes   It would be
distressing to See our Situation, all wet and Colde our
bedding also wet, (and the robes of the party which
Compose half the bedding is rotten and we are not in
a Situation to supply their places) in a wet bottom
Scercely large enough to contain us, our baggage half
a mile from us and Canoes at the mercy of the waves,
altho Secured as well as possible, Sunk with emence
parcels of Stone to wate them down to prevent their
dashing to pieces against the rocks; one got loose last
night and was left on a rock a Short distance below,
without rciving more dammage than a Split in her

bottom — Fortunately for us our men are healthy. 3
men Gibson Bratten & Willard attempted to go
around the point below in our Indian Canoe, much
Such a canoe as the Indians visited us in yesterday,
they proceeded to the point from which they were
oblige to return, the waves tossing them about at will
I walked up the branch and giged 3 Salmon trout. the
party killed 13 Salmon to day in a branch about 2
miles above. rain Continued —WILLIAM CLARK

Nearing the mouth of the Columbia River the expedition was overcome by fierce Pacific storms, high waves
and huge trees falling all around them. After being "at
the mercy of waves & driftwood," they took refuge in
this bay.

73

Abandoned experimental
jet boat, Hungry
Harbor, washington

"Ocian 4142 Miles from the Mouth of Missouri R"

74

NOVEMBER 15, 1805

I told those Indians . . . that they Should not Come near us, and if any one of their nation Stold anything from us, I would have him Shot, which they understoot verry well. —WILLIAM CLARK

In 1788 a British merchant, Captain John Meares, had named the tip of land that the Corps of Discovery finally reached "Cape Disappointment." For Lewis too the land held only disappointment; it not only lacked game but also failed to produce the white traders who, he'd been told, lived here. Lewis searched nine miles in a northerly direction around the tip but then returned and set up camp, protected from the howling winds and pounding surf of the Pacific. While Lewis explored Cape Disappointment, two of his men camped with the Indians, who stole their rifles. Lewis threatened force in a bluff and recovered their guns. He sent the group back to Clark who, perhaps because of the miserable conditions of constant cold and wet, exploded in anger. Later the two captains carved their names on a tree, with Clark adding, "by land from the U States in 1805 & 1806."

75

campsite, chinook
point, washington

An old woman & wife to a Cheif of the <u>Chinnooks</u> came and made a Camp near ours   She brought with her 6 young Squars . . . <u>her daughters</u> & <u>nieces</u> . . . I believe for the purpose of gratifying the passions of the men of our party and receiving for those indulgiences Such Small as She (the old woman) thought proper to accept of, Those people appear to view Sensuality as a Necessary evel, and do not appear to abhor it as a Crime in the unmarried State— . . . the womin of the Chinnook Nation have handsom faces low and badly made with large legs & thighs which are generally Swelled from a Stopage of the circulation in the feet (which are Small) by maney Strands of Beeds or curious Strings which are drawn tight around the leg above the anckle, their legs are also picked with different figures, I Saw on the left arm of a Squar the following letters <u>J. Bowmon</u> —WILLIAM CLARK

Chinook Point was the farthest point west that the expedition's canoes could advance against the relentless storms, and they camped here for close to a week. At Chinook Point they took a vote whether to abandon the north shore and cross over to the south in search of winter quarters. Every person, including Sacagawea and York, Clark's black slave, had an equal voice.

DECEMBER 25, 1805

at day light this morning we we[re] awoke by the discharge of the fire arm of all our party & a Selute, Shoute and a Song which the whole party joined in under our windows . . . were Chearfull all the morning—after brackfast we divided our Tobacco which amounted to 12 carrots one half of which we gave to the men of the party who used tobacco, and to those who doe not use it we make a present of a handkerchief. . . . I recved a presnt of Capt L. of a fleece hosrie Shirt Draws and Socks—, a pr. mockersons of Whitehouse a Small Indian basket of Gutherich, two Dozen white weazils tails of the Indian woman. . . . The day proved Showerey wet and disagreeable.

we would have Spent this day the nativity of Christ in feasting, had we any thing either to raise our Sperits or even gratify our appetites, our Diner concisted of pore Elk, So much Spoiled that we eate it thro' mear necessity, Some Spoiled pounded fish and a fiew roots. —WILLIAM CLARK

The Corps passed their second winter here in miserable conditions: rain coming down every day "except twelve," fleas infesting their bedding, clothes rotting off their backs, and spoiled food their only sustenance. Adding to their problems, their supply of trade goods was running low, and the Clatsop Indians were savvy traders from their experience with the British and expected reasonable payment.

A community-built replica of Fort Clatsop, now a national memorial run by the National Park Service, stands about four miles from the Pacific where the Netul River enters the bay at Astoria. The replica is fifty-feet square with two long, facing buildings connected by a high fence and the parade ground in the center. Small rooms in each building provided quarters for the enlisted men on one side, and on the other, for the captains, the Charbonneaus, a smoke house, and an orderly room.

Archaeologists continue to work at Fort Clatsop, in part to establish the location of the original fort. The site for the replica was based on the journals and local accounts, but nothing remained at the site to indicate the spot. Researchers hoped to help pinpoint the location by finding the fort's latrine by looking for mercury compounds in the soil, the last traces of Lewis's treatments for dysentery and venereal disease, but the tests proved inconclusive as there were conflicting interpretations of the results. They've also used high-tech magnetometer surveys to search for artifacts left at Fort Clatsop by the Corps of Discovery, but there, too, have not met with unqualified success. Interestingly, though the expedition established more than six hundred campsites, only one has been confirmed definitively with physical evidence, Lower Portage on the Missouri River in Montana.

76

fort clatsop National
Memorial, astoria,
oregon

our party from necessaty having been obliged to sub-sist some lenth of time on dogs have now become extreemly fond of their flesh; it is worthy of remark that while we lived principally on the flesh of this anamal we were much more healthy strong and more fleshey than we had been since we left the Buffaloe country. for my own part I have become so perfectly reconciled to the dog that I think it an agreeable food and would prefer it vastly to lean Venison or Elk.

—MERIWETHER LEWIS

In the distance is the point of land that Clark named Point William, after himself. The Corps of Discovery camped in Point William's low notch while they searched both sides of the estuary for a suitable location for their winter fort. They chose the bank on the right (the south bank of the Columbia River) to build their fort because the Indians reported that more deer and elk could be found there. In reality, there was very little game to be had, and the expedition survived mostly on dog meat and rotten salmon that they obtained by trading with the Clatsop Indians and on elk (of poor quality) that they hunted far from the vicinity of Fort Clatsop. Point William had another name—Tongue Point—before Lewis and Clark arrived, and that is what it's still called today.

77

pilings and point william, Bay of Astoria, oregon

JANUARY 8, 1806

The kil a mox although they possessed large quantities of this blubber and oil were so prenurious that they disposed of it with great reluctiance and in Small quantities only; insomuch that my utmost exertion aided by the party with the Small Stock of merchindize I had taken with me were not able to precure more blubber than about 300 wt. and a fiew gallons of oil; Small as this Stock is I prise it highly; and thank providence for directing the whale to us; and think him much more kind to us than he was to jonah, having Sent this monster to be swallowed by us in Sted of swallowing of us as jonah's did.

JANUARY 9, 1806

we have now to look back and Shudder at the dreadfull road on which we have to return of 45 miles S E of Point adams & 35 miles from Fort Catsop. I had the blubber & oil divided among' the party and Set out about Sunrise and returned by the Same rout we had went out, met Several parties of men & womin of the Chinnook and Clatsops nations, on their way to trade with the kil a mox for blubber and oil; on the Steep decent of the Mountain I overtook five men and Six womin with emence loads of the Oil and blubber of the Whale, those Indians had passed by Some rout by which we missed them as we went out

yesterday; one of the women in the act of getting down a Steep part of the mountain her load by Some means had Sliped off her back, and She was holding the load by a Strap which was fastened to the mat bag in which it was in, in one hand and holding a bush by the other, as I was in front of my party, I endeavored to relieve this woman by takeing her load untill She Could get to a better place a little below, & to my estonishment found the load as much as I Could lift and must exceed 100 wt. the husband of this woman who was below Soon came to her relief.

—WILLIAM CLARK

As soon as Clark had received the report of a beached whale, he set out, hoping to trade for blubber. With him went six men and Sacagawea with her baby. They followed an Indian guide and climbed over the steep Tillamook Headlands, reaching what is now called Cannon Beach, seventeen miles from Fort Clatsop. By the time they arrived, a skeleton was all that was left of the whale, and the Indians were boiling the remaining blubber for oil.

79

JANUARY 5, 1806

At 5 p. m. Willard and Wiser returned, they had not been lost as we expected. they informd us that it was not untill the 5th day after leaving the fort, that they Could find a Convenient place for makeing Salt; that they had at length established themselves on the Sea Coast about 15 miles S. W. from this, near the houses of Some Clat Sop & Kil a mox families; that the Indians were very friendly and had given them a considerable quantity of the blubber of the whale which perished on the Coast. . . . we had part of it Cooked and found it very pallitable and tender, it resembles the beaver in flavour. . . . they Commenced the makeing of Salt and found that they Could make from 3 quarts to a gallon a day. . . . this Salt was a great treat to most of the party, haveing not had any Since the 20 th ulto. as to my Self I care but little whether I have any with my meat or not; provided the meat fat, haveing from habit become entirely cearless about my diat, and I have learned to think that if the Cord be Sufficiently Strong which binds the Soul and boddy together, it does not So much matter about the materials which Compose it. —WILLIAM CLARK

In determining a location for their winter fort, Lewis wanted proximity to the ocean so that they could produce salt for the return trip, and for trading with the coastal Indians. Clark found a suitable site with access to sea water, wood for the fires, and game to hunt for food. The site was also selected with an eye toward keeping a watch for a trading vessel from which the expedition could restock their supplies. That winter they produced four or five bushels of salt.

The persons who usually visit the entrance of this river for the purpose of traffic or hunting I believe are either English or Americans; the Indians inform us that they speak the same language with ourselves, and give us proofs of their varacity by repeating many words of English, as musquit, powder, shot, nife, file, damned rascal, sun of a bitch &c. whether these traders are from Nootka sound, from some other late establishment on this coast, or immediately from the U' States or Great Brittain, I am at a loss to determine, nor can the Indians inform us. . . . This traffic on the part of the whites consists in vending, guns, (principally old british or American musquits) powder, balls and Shot, Copper and brass kettles, brass teakettles and coffee pots, blankets from two to three point, scarlet and blue Cloth (coarse), plates and strips of sheet copper and brass, large brass wire, knives, beads and tobacco with fishinghooks buttons and some other small articles; also a considerable quantity of Sailor's cloaths, as hats coats, trowsers and shirts. for these they receive in return from the natives, dressed and undressed Elkskins, skins of the sea Otter, common Otter, beaver, common fox, spuck, and tiger cat; also dried and pounded sammon in baskets, and a kind of buisquit, which the natives make of roots called by them shappelell. —MERIWETHER LEWIS

Lewis was desperate to resupply his stock for trading with the Indians. They were almost out of trinkets and willing to barter the clothes off their backs in exchange for food. Lewis also wanted to send back copies of his journals. For an entire year, since their winter at Fort Mandan, they had been out of communication, and he had no certainty of their safe return home. Facing the mouth of the Columbia estuary, the beachhead was a logical place to spot a ship. Lewis was carrying a letter of credit backed by the United States treasury to use for trade with any vessel they encountered on the West Coast, but he searched in vain.

80

wreck of the peter iredale, near fort clatsop, washington

The Return Journey

{ 164 }

MARCH 20, 1806

It continued to rain and blow so violently to day that nothing could be done towards forwarding our departure. . . .

Altho' we have not fared Sumptuously this winter & spring at Fort Clatsop, we have lived quit as comfortably as we had any reason to expect we Should; and have accomplished every object which induced our remaining at this place except that of meeting with the traders who visit the entrance of this river. our salt will be very sufficient to last us to the Missouri where we have a Stock in Store. . . .

maney of our men are Still Complaining of being unwell; Bratten and Willard remain weak principally I beleive for the want of proper food. I expect when we get under way that we Shall be much more healthy. it has always had that effect on us heretofore.

—MERIWETHER LEWIS

At the Pacific Ocean, Clark had calculated the journey back to the mouth of the Missouri to be 4,142 miles (he was off by only 40 miles), and while waiting at Fort Clatsop for winter's end, the captains concocted a daring plan for their return trip. After they had crossed back over the Bitterroots, they decided they would split the group at the Travelers' Rest campsite. Lewis and nine men would explore north along the Marias River to find its source. (The Louisiana Purchase included all the water drainage land east and north of the Rocky Mountains, and the U.S. and Canadian border would be determined by how far north the water drained into the Missouri basin.) They would travel on horseback, taking an overland shortcut to reach the Great Falls. There Lewis's group would split again, with Lewis taking three men to explore the Marias, leaving six behind to help with portage.

Meanwhile Clark and the rest of the men would return on horseback over Lemhi Pass and the Continental Divide to Camp Fortunate where they would retrieve the sunken canoes and cached supplies left behind on the outbound journey. Here Clark, too, would divide his party, and with ten men he would ride east with the herd of horses and find the Yellowstone River. Clark's group would then follow the Yellowstone, exploring across what is today the state of Montana until, as they had learned the year before, it joined with the Missouri River. The rest of Clark's men would refloat the canoes, dig up the hidden supplies, and navigate downstream to the Great Falls where they would rejoin Lewis's men and together portage around the falls. Once around the falls, this group expected to meet Lewis upon his return from his mission to the north, and together they would canoe downstream on the Missouri to its confluence with the Yellowstone River where they would meet up with Clark's party. Before they could put their complicated plan into action, however, they needed to recover the horses they had left with the Nez Perce. They spent almost two weeks getting up the river on their way to get the horses, and experienced trouble with the Indians in the area along the way.

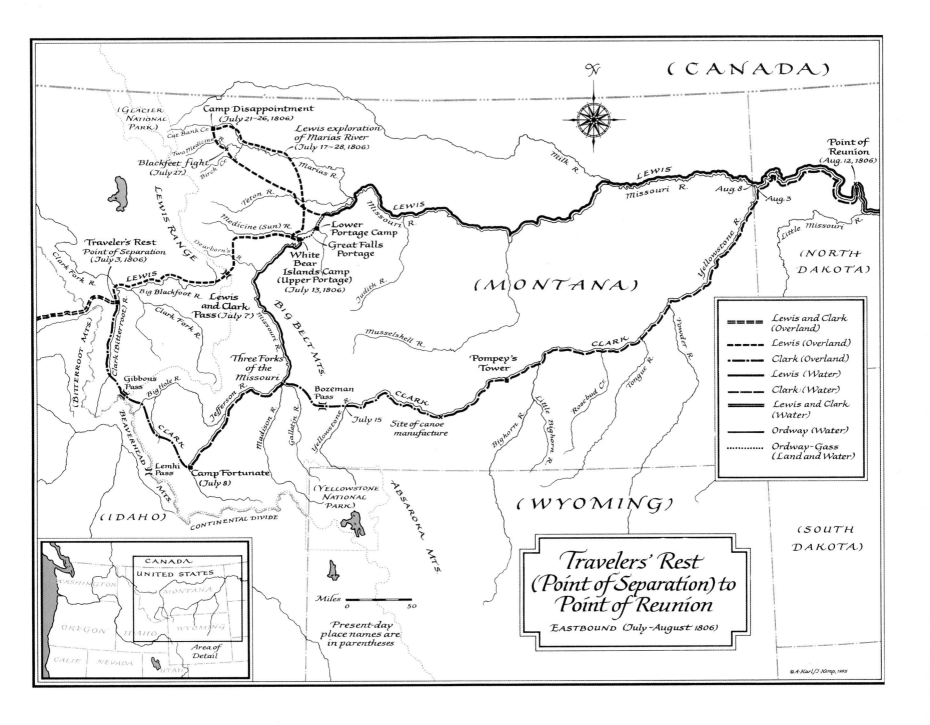

(CANADA)

N

(GLACIER NATIONAL PARK)

Camp Disappointment
(July 21–26, 1806)

Lewis exploration
of Marias River
(July 17–28, 1806)

Cut Bank Cr.

Two Medicine R.

Blackfeet fight
(July 27)

Birch Cr.

Marias R.

Milk R.

LEWIS

Point of
Reunion
(Aug. 12, 1806)

Teton R.

LEWIS

Missouri R.

Aug. 8

Aug. 3

LEWIS RANGE

Medicine (Sun) R.

Lower
Portage Camp

Great Falls
Portage

Missouri R.

Little Missouri R.

Traveler's Rest
Point of Separation
(July 3, 1806)

Dearborn's R.

White
Bear
Islands Camp
(Upper Portage)
(July 13, 1806)

(NORTH
DAKOTA)

Clark Fork R.

LEWIS

Big Blackfoot R.

Lewis
and Clark
Pass (July 7)

Missouri R.

BIG BELT MTS.

Judith R.

Yellowstone R.

(MONTANA)

Clark Fork R.

Musselshell R.

BITTERROOT MTS.

Clark (Bitterroot) R.

CLARK

Three Forks
of the
Missouri

Jefferson R.

Bozeman
Pass

CLARK

Pompey's
Tower

CLARK

Powder R.

Gibbons
Pass

Big Hole R.

Madison R.

Gallatin R.

Yellowstone R.

July 15

Site of canoe
manufacture

Bighorn R.

Little Bighorn R.

Rosebud Cr.

Tongue R.

BEAVERHEAD MTS.

CLARK

Lemhi
Pass

Camp Fortunate
(July 8)

(YELLOWSTONE
NATIONAL
PARK)

ABSAROKA MTS.

(WYOMING)

(IDAHO)

CONTINENTAL DIVIDE

Legend:
- - - - Lewis and Clark (Overland)
- - - - Lewis (Overland)
-·-·- Clark (Overland)
——— Lewis (Water)
– – – Clark (Water)
━━━ Lewis and Clark (Water)
——— Ordway (Water)
·········· Ordway-Gass (Land and Water)

(SOUTH
DAKOTA)

Miles
0   50

Present-day
place names are
in parentheses

Travelers' Rest
(Point of Separation) to
Point of Reunion

EASTBOUND (July–August 1806)

Inset map:
CANADA
UNITED STATES
WASHINGTON
OREGON
IDAHO
MONTANA
WYOMING
CALIF.
NEVADA
UTAH
Area of
Detail

© A. Karl / J. Kemp, 1995

81

MARCH 17, 1806

Drewyer returned late this evening from the Cathlah-mahs with our canoe which Sergt. Pryor had left some days since, and also a canoe which he had purchased from those people. for this canoe he gave my uniform laced coat and nearly half a carrot of tobacco. it seems that nothing excep this coat would induce them to dispose of a canoe which in their mode of traffic is an article of the greatest val[u]e except a wife, with whom it is equal, and is generally given in exchange to the father for his daughter. I think the U' States are indebted to me another Uniform coat, for that of which I have disposed on this occasion was but little woarn.— we yet want another canoe, and as the Clatsops will not sell us one at a price which we can afford to give we will take one from them in lue of the six Elk which they stole from us in the winter.

—MERIWETHER LEWIS

On March 23 the Corps of Discovery left Fort Clatsop and started back up the Columbia. As they passed what is now Longview, their supplies were almost depleted. Lewis had written before they set off that "two hand-kercheifs would now contain all the small articles of merchandize which we possess." They planned to canoe the Columbia to the falls area, where they would trade for horses, but they were desperate for another canoe. They stole a canoe from a Clatsop Indian and justified the theft by claiming the Indians had taken six elk from them during the winter. An Indian guide later said that the canoe was his, but intimidated by thirty-two armed men, he accepted an elk hide in payment. Once they passed through the Columbia River Gorge, they planned to dig up the trade goods buried between Nez Perce country and the Great Falls to get them home.

APRIL 1, 1806

We were visited by several canoes of natives in the course of the day; most of whom were decending the river with their women and children. they informed us that they resided at the great rapids and that their relations at that place were much streightened at that place for the want of food; that they had consumed their winter store of dryed fish and that those of the present season had not yet arrived. I could not learn wheather they took the Sturgeon but presume if they do it is in but small quantities as they complained much of the scarcity of food among them. they informed us that the nations above them were in the same situation & that they did not expect the Salmon to arrive untill the full of the next moon which happens on the 2d of May. we did not doubt the varacity of these people who seemed to be on their way with their families and effects in surch of subsistence which they find it easy to procure in this fertile valley.— This information gave us much uneasiness with rispect to our future means of subsistence.

APRIL 3, 1806

these poor people appeared to be almost starved, they picked up the bones and little peices of refuse meat which had been thrown away by the party.

—MERIWETHER LEWIS

The Corps of Discovery was struggling upstream, bucking a steady current, portaging around falls, and towing canoes over rapids. Lewis learned about food shortages upriver, but he did not want to delay the trip for another month by waiting for the salmon to run. Game was scarce, and the men would have to live on dog meat while they were below The Dalles, and on horse meat after they had crossed the mountains. The modern fish ladder around Bonneville Dam was installed to enable salmon to navigate upriver during spawning season.

APRIL 24, 1806

we now sold our canoes for a few strands of beads. . . .
the natives had tantalized us with an exchange of
horses for our canoes in the first instance, but when
they found that we had made our arrangements to
travel by land they would give us nothing for them I
determined to cut them in peices sooner than leave
them on those terms, Drewyer struck one of the
canoes and split of a small peice with his tomma-
hawk, they discovered us determined on this subject
and offered us several strands of beads for each which
were accepted. —MERIWETHER LEWIS

After the expedition had traveled about two hundred
miles up the Columbia River, they left their canoes
behind and traveled on horses. While they had successfully traded for some horses, they needed more. The
Indians near The Dalles were shrewd traders and recognized quickly their advantage over the travelers. They
refused to accept what Clark offered (and it was in reality little). After several days of haggling, Lewis finally
agreed to pay the price of two large, valuable cooking
kettles in exchange for four horses. All the way along
the Columbia, the Indians continued to steal from
them, greatly upsetting Lewis, who, after obtaining
the final ten horses, had a canoe put on the fire and
burned "so that not a particle should be left for the
benefit of the Indians." Even as the canoe was burning,
another Indian was discovered stealing a piece of iron,
and Lewis caught and beat him severely.

83

power lines along the
columbia river gorge,
looking east, near
wishram, washington

83

84

cape horn on the
columbia river, near
washougal, washington

APRIL 11, 1806

three of this same tribe of villains the Wah-clel-lars, stole my dog this evening, and took him towards their village; I was shortly afterwards informed of this transaction by an indian who spoke the Clatsop language . . . and sent three men in pursuit of the theives with orders if they made the least resistence or difficulty in surrendering the dog to fire on them; they overtook these fellows or reather came within sight of them at the distance of about 2 miles; the indians discovering the party in pursuit of them left the dog and fled. they also stole an ax from us, but scarcely had it their possession before Thompson detected them and wrest it from them. we ordered the centinel to keep them out of camp, and informed them by signs that if they made any further attempts to steal our property or insulted our men we should put them to instant death. a cheif of the Clah-clel-lah tribe informed us that there were two very bad men among the Wah-clel-lahs who had been the principal actors in these seenes of outradge of which we complained, and that it was not the wish of the nation by any means to displease us. we told him that we hoped it might be the case, but we should certainly be as good as our words if they presisted in their insolence. I am convinced that no other consideration but our number at this moment protects us.

—MERIWETHER LEWIS

Lewis's prized dog, a Newfoundland named Seaman, had accompanied him the entire way, and Lewis went into a rage when the dog was stolen by Chinook Indians. His fury worked against a primary goal of the expedition— to convince the Indians of the benevolence and peacefulness of their new white father. Lewis mentioned Seaman frequently in his diaries until July 15, 1806, when the dog disappeared from the record. This incident occurred near what is called Cape Horn, an outcropping of rocks on a point of land along the Columbia River just east of present-day Portland, Oregon. This view is from the Washington side of the river.

APRIL 28, 1806

This morning early Yellept brought a very eligant white horse to our camp and presented him to Capt. C. signifying his wish to get a kettle but on being informed that we had already disposed of every kettle we could possibly spear he said he was content with whatever he thought proper to give him. Capt. C. gave him his swoard . . . a hundred balls and powder and some sall articles with which he appeared perfectly satisfied. . . . being anxious to depart we requested the Cheif to furnish us with canoes to pass the river, but he insisted on our remaining with him this day at least, that he would be much pleased if we would conset to remain two or three, but he would not let us have canoes to leave him today. that he had sent for the Chym nâp'-pos his neighbours to come down and join his people this evening and dance for us. . . . a little before sunset the Chymnahpos arrived; they were about 100 men and a few women; they joined the Wallahwollahs who were about the same number and formed a half circle arround our camp where they waited very patiently to see our party dance. the fiddle was played and the men amused themselves with dancing about an hour. we then requested the Indians to dance which they very cheerfully complyed with.

MAY 1, 1806

some time after we had encamped three young men arrived from the Wallahwollah village bringing with them a steel trap belonging to one of our party which had been neglegently left behind; this is an act of integrity rarely witnessed among indians. during our stay with them they several times found the knives of the men which had been carelessly lossed by them and returned them. I think we can justly affirm to the honor of these people that they are the most hospitable, honest, and sincere people that we have met with in our voyage. —MERIWETHER LEWIS

At the junction of the two rivers, the Corps encountered the Walla Walla Indians and Chief Yelleppit, whom they had earlier met on their outbound journey. Because they had burned their last canoe, they needed canoes to carry their baggage across the Columbia River to reach the opposite shore where the Walla Walla River entered. They intended to take the Nez Perce trail overland, following the Walla Walla River and a series of tributary creeks, until they reached what is today Lewiston, Idaho. This route eliminated what would have been a dangerous upstream journey against the torrents of the Snake River.

85

MOUTH OF THE WALLA WALLA RIVER AT THE COLUMBIA RIVER, LOOKING EAST, WALLULA, WASHINGTON

MAY 5, 1806

while at dinner an indian fellow very impertinently
threw a half Starved puppy nearly into the plate of
Capt. Lewis by way of derision for our eating dogs
and laughed very heartily at his own impertinence;
Capt L.— was So provoked at the insolence that he
cought the puppy and threw it with great violence at
him and Struck him in the breast and face, Seazed
his tomahawk, and Shewed him by Sign that if he
repeeted his insolence that he would tomahawk him,
the fellow withdrew apparently much mortified and
we continued our Dinner without further
Molestation. —WILLIAM CLARK

The expedition camped in the land of the Nez Perce
Nation at a site near the center of the photograph
where a small grove of trees circles Pataha Creek. Their
supply of useful trade goods was now depleted. They
survived by bartering medical services for food and fuel
from the Indians. When they first passed through this
region, Clark had, with great ceremony, cured a man
who had not walked for months by rubbing an oint-
ment into his legs. While it was unlikely that the salve
had caused his miraculous recovery, the captain gained
a reputation for powerful medicine among the Nez
Perce, confirmed by another effective solution that
Clark applied to their eyes. The cures may have been
little more than placebos, but the captains were willing
"to continue this deseption for they will not give us any
provision withhout compensation in merchandize and
our stock is now reduced to a mere handfull. we take
care to give them no article which can possibly oinjure
them." Still, Clark's medicine was not enough to obtain
food for the entire group, and the men were soon bartering their shirts and trouser buttons for food. By the
time the Corps set off, they had managed to accumu-
late a herd of sixty-five horses, enough for the return
trip over the dreaded Bitterroot Mountains.

86

campsite, touchet
river, near dayton,
washington

87

couple and overheated
truck, near Touchet
River, washington

JUNE 17, 1806

we left . . . our instruments papers &c beleiving them safer here than to wrisk them on horseback over the roads and creeks which we had passed. our baggage being laid on scaffoalds and well covered we began our retrograde march at 1 P. M. having remained about 3 hours on this snowey mountain. we returned by the rout we had come to hungry creek, which we ascended about 2 miles and encamped. we had here more grass for our horses than the preceeding evening yet it was but scant. the party were a good deel dejected tho' not so as I had apprehended they would have been. this is the first time since we have been on this long tour that we have ever been compelled to retreat or make a retrograde march. —MERIWETHER LEWIS

The hillside in the background bears scars of the two Indian trails followed by the Corps when they took the shortcut to the Snake River. They expected to reach the Bitterroot Mountains quickly and then recross the Lolo Trail, but the trail was blocked by snow. The Indians refused to guide them until it melted. The men camped and waited for a month, but Lewis grew increasingly impatient to cross the mountains and they started out without a guide. After a couple of days the party encountered snow packs ten- to fifteen-feet deep and were forced to return. Facing seemingly insurmountable difficulties, Lewis decided to offer three new-model army rifles and ten horses—an unprecedented payment—to any Indian who would guide them over the mountains. Three Indians took the offer and led the Corps over the 156-mile trail in six days, almost half the time it had taken the expedition the year before. The way was treacherous, even without snow, and Lewis's horse fell backward off the steep, rocky trail, almost crushing Lewis as they slid forty feet down the mountain. Miraculously, both man and animal escaped injury.

JUNE 29, 1806

*in this bath which had been prepared by the Indians by stopping the river with Stone and mud, I bathed and remained in 10 minits it was with dificuelty I could remain this long and it causd a profuse swet. . . . we think the temperature of those Springs about the Same as that of the hotest of the hot Springs of Virginia. both the Men and the indians amused themselves with the use of the bath this evening. I observe after the indians remaining in the hot bath as long as they could bear it run and plunge themselves into the Creek the water of which is now as Cold as ice Can make it; after remaining here a fiew minits they return again to the worm bath repeeting this transision Several times but always ending with the worm bath. Saw the tracks of 2 bearfooted Indians. —*WILLIAM CLARK

JULY 3, 1806

I took leave of my worthy friend and companion Capt. Clark and the party that accompanyed him. I could not avoid feeling much concern on this occasion although I hoped this seperation was only momentary.

—MERIWETHER LEWIS

Located on the eastern slope of the Bitterroots, the hot springs were close to the Travelers' Rest campground where the Corps was heading with plans to divide into two groups. The separation would last for six weeks, with Lewis traveling eight hundred miles, and Clark a thousand, through unknown Indian country.

88

lolo Hot springs,
montana

89

vandalized monument
to Lewis, Blackfeet
Indian Reservation,
near Browning, Montana

This monument marks the northern-most point of Lewis's three-day journey up the Marias River. He had taken every north-branching fork, hoping eventually to reach 50 degrees northern latitude, and was on Cut Bank Creek, which drains out of present-day Glacier National Park. Because the creek flowed due east, Lewis knew that he had reached the northern end of the Louisiana Purchase. The Canadian border thereby remained at 48 degrees. They made camp here for several days, and Lewis named their turnaround campsite Camp Disappointment.

I pursued the man who had taken my gun who with another was driving off a part of the horses which were to the left of the camp, I pursued them so closely that they could not take twelve of their own horses but continued to drive one of mine with some others; at the distance of three hundred paces they entered one of those steep nitches in the bluff with the horses before them   being nearly out of breath I could pursue no further, I called to them as I had done several times before that I would shoot them if they did not give me my horse and raised my gun, one of them jumped behind a rock and spoke to the other who turned arround and stoped at the distance of 30 steps from me and I shot him through the belly, he fell to his knees and on his wright elbow from which position he partly raised himself up and fired at me, and turning himself about crawled in behind a rock which was a few feet from him. he overshot me, being bearheaded I felt the wind of his bullet very distinctly.

—MERIWETHER LEWIS

Heading back down the Marias River, Lewis camped at Two Medicine River, and here in the middle of what is now the Blackfeet Indian Reservation a serious conflict erupted. Lewis and three men encountered a group of young Blackfeet and nervously shared camp with them. (Their camp is believed to have been located in the fenced area in the center of the photograph.) Lewis told the Blackfeet of his success in securing peace and trade with the tribes on both sides of the Rocky Mountains. He invited the Blackfeet to join them, but the Blackfeet were already trading partners with the British, and their superiority over other tribes depended on their having sole access to guns through the British. They did not welcome the prospect of other tribes challenging their position. Perhaps it was this startling information or merely the opportunity for an easy robbery that encouraged the young Indians to attempt to steal the expedition's rifles and horses. Awakened by noises in the early dawn, Lewis and his men struggled to prevent the theft. Their resistance ended with two Indians killed. The men made a hasty retreat down the Marias, covering a hundred miles in about twenty-four hours. When they reached the Missouri River, yet another miraculous coincidence awaited them—they ran into the men traveling by canoe, who were coming down the river after having portaged the Great Falls.

90

site of fight with Blackfeet Indians, near Cut Bank, Montana

91

cloud over bozeman
pass, main street,
bozeman, montana

JULY 13, 1806

Set out early this morning and proceded on very well to the enterance of Madicines river at our old Encampment of the 27th July last . . . where I found Sergt. Pryor and party with the horses, they had arrived at this place one hour before us. his party had killed 6 deer & a white bear   I had all the horses driven across Madicine & gallitines rivers and halted to dine and let the horses feed imediately below the enterance of Gallitine. had all the baggage of the land party taken out of the Canoes and after dinner the 6 Canoes and the party of 10 men under the direction of Sergt. Ordway Set out. the horses feet are very sore and Several of them can Scaercely proceed on. . . . at 5 P.M I Set out from the head of Missouri at the 3 forks, and proceeded on. . . . Saw a large Gange of Elk in the plains and Deer in the river bottoms. Gibson killed an otter the fur of which was much longer and whiter than any which I had Seen. . . . all the meat I had put into the Canoes except a Sufficiency for Supper. The Country in the forks between Gallitins & Madisens rivers is a butifull leavel plain Covered with low grass. . . . The Indian woman who has been of great Service to me as a pilot through this country recommends a gap in the mountain more South which I shall cross.

—WILLIAM CLARK

Clark's group was on horseback heading east along the Gallatin River, working their way upriver to a pass that would take them to the Yellowstone. Historians have speculated about Sacagawea's value as a guide. She had been captured as a child and taken eight hundred miles from her western homeland to live with the Mandans, and it is thought that she knew very little about the Missouri east of the Rocky Mountains, and even less about the west. Most likely the Yellowstone River was close enough to her birthplace to be familiar, allowing her to recall a mountain pass east of present-day Bozeman.

JULY 21, 1806

This morning I was informed that Half of our horses were absent. . . . I deturmined to have the ballance of the horses guarded and for that purpose sent out 3 men, on their approach near the horses were So alarmed that they ran away and entered the woods

JULY 22, 1806

I Sent Sergt. Pryor and Shabono in Serch of the horses with directions to proceed up the river as far as the 1st narrows and examine particularly for their tracks, they returned at 3 P M and informed me that they had proceeded up the distance I derected them to go and could See neither horses nor tracks; the Plains imediately out from Camp is So dry and hard that the track of a horse Cannot be Seen without close examination. . . . begin to Suspect that they are taken by the Indians and taken over the hard plains to prevent our following them. my Suspicions is grounded on the improbility of the horses leaving the grass and rushes of the river bottoms of which they are very fond, and takeing imediately out into the open dry plains where the grass is but Short and dry.

JULY 23, 1806

Sgt. pryor found an Indian Mockerson and a Small piece of a roab, the mockerson worn out on the bottom & yet wet, and have every appearance of haveing been worn but a fiew hours before. those Indian Signs

is Conclusive with me that they have taken the 24 horses which we lost on the night of the 20th instant, and that those who were about last night were in Serch of the ballance of our horses which they could not find as they had fortunately got into a Small Prarie Serounded with thick timber in the bottom.
—WILLIAM CLARK

Clark planned to take nine men, Sacagawea, and fifty horses downstream along the Yellowstone River to the Mandan Villages in North Dakota where he intended to trade the horses for supplies from a British trader whom they had met the year before. He assigned three men to drive the horses while the rest of the party went ahead in their newly made canoes. Just east of present-day Columbus, Montana, the Crow Indians, who were the most skillful and invisible horse thieves on the Plains, stole twenty-four horses. By the time the group driving the remaining twenty-six horses reached the country in what is now the city of Billings, their horses had also gone missing. Clark was not to receive this unsettling news until he again met up with the men responsible for tending the horses. Once the horses were gone, the men continued their journey in bull boats and followed days behind Clark all the way to the junction with the Missouri where the two groups finally caught up with each other.

92

site where the horses were stolen, near columbus, Montana

JULY 24, 1806

for me to mention or give an estimate of the differant Spcies of wild animals on this river particularly Buffalow, Elk Antelopes & Wolves would be increditable. I shall therefore be silent on the Subject further.
—WILLIAM CLARK

During their journey down the Yellowstone River, Clark mentions no contact with Indians, although they saw smoke signals, most likely coming from fires of the Crow tribe. Shortly before reaching this point, where the Yellowstone flows through present-day Billings, Private George Gibson fell off his horse and a sharp branch pierced his thigh. An infection set in, reducing his ability to ride to only a couple of hours a day, and Clark decided to make canoes earlier than planned. They lashed two dugouts together for stability. As they passed through this valley, now a major agricultural area, they saw buffalo, deer, elk, bears, and pronghorns so plentiful that even Clark, who by now had seen extraordinary quantities of animal and plant life in the territory, was overwhelmed by their abundance.

93

Yellowstone River,
Billings, Montana

94

AUGUST 7, 1806

at 4 P.M. we arrived at the entrance of the Yellowstone river. I landed at the point and found that Capt. Clark had been encamped at this place and . . . from appearances had left it about 7 or 8 days. I found a paper on a pole at the point which mearly contained my name in the hand wrighting of Capt. C. we also found the remnant of a note which been attached to a peace of Elk's horns in the camp; from this fragment I learned that game was scarce at the point and musquetoes troublesome which were the reasons given for his going on; I also learnt that he intended halting a few miles below where he intended waiting my arrival. I now wrote a note directed to Colter and Collins provided they were behind, order-ing them to come on without loss of time; this note I wraped in leather and attatced onto the same pole which Capt. C. had planted at the point; this being done I instantly reimbarked and decended the river in the hope of reaching Capt. C's camp before night.

—MERIWETHER LEWIS

From this point, looking north along the Yellowstone, it is only five miles to the junction with the Missouri River. Clark and his small party were in canoes here and had floated nearly three hundred miles across the current state of Montana. Unknown to Clark, the remainder of his party followed in the bull boats. Amazingly, within a week of each other, all three groups—Clark, the horse-drivers, and Lewis—came together near the confluence of the Yellowstone and Missouri. The single pier in the river is all that remains of an old bridge.

I was in the act of firing on the Elk a second time when a ball struck my left thye about an inch below my hip joint, missing the bone it passed through the left thye and cut the thickness of the bullet across the hinder part of the right thye; the stroke was very severe; I instantly supposed that Cruzatte had shot me in mistake for an Elk as I was dressed in brown leather and he cannot see very well; under this impression I called out to him damn you, you have shot me, and looked towards the place from whence the ball had come, seeing nothing I called Cruzatte several times as loud as I could but received no answer; I was now preswaded that it was an indian that had shot me . . . in this situation not knowing how many indians there might be concealed in the bushes I thought best to make good my retreat to the perogue. . . . when I arrived in sight of the perogue I called the men to their arms to which they flew in an instant . . . the men followed me as they were bid and I returned about a hundred paces when my wounds became so painfull and my thye so stiff that I could scarcely get on. . . . the party returned with Cruzatte and reported that there were no indians nor the appearance of any; Cruzatte seemed much allarmed and declared if he had shot me it was not his intention. . . . I do not beleive that the fellow did it intentionally but after finding that he had shot me was anxious to conceal his knowledge of having done so. . . . as it was painfull to me to be removed I slept on board the perogue; the pain I experienced excited a high fever and I had a very uncomfortable night.

—MERIWETHER LEWIS

Four days after he left the countryside near the site where Fort Union would be built twenty-three years later, Lewis was shot. In 1828 Fort Union was built at the junction of the Missouri and Yellowstone Rivers as a trading hub for John Astor's American Fur Company. Five years later, Prince Maximilian of Weid, Prussia, with his artist Karl Bodmer, arrived at Fort Union on a steamboat. In 1833, the year of his visit, Maximilian reported that the company shipped downriver to St. Louis 42,000 buffalo hides valued at $168,000 and another 35,000 hides of more exotic animals such as beaver, mink, weasel, and red fox. For a period of time the fort supported a lavish lifestyle for its company executives. It was torn down in the 1860s.

95

Approaching reconstructed Fort Union, near Williston, North Dakota

96

confluence of
Missouri and
Yellowstone Rivers,
Fort Buford,
North Dakota

AUGUST 12, 1806

at meridian Capt Lewis hove in Sight with the party which went by way of the Missouri as well as that which accompanied him from Travellers rest on Clarks river; I was alarmed on the landing of the Canoes to be informed that Capt. Lewis was wounded by an accident —. I found him lying in the Perogue, he informed me that his wound was slight and would be well in 20 or 30 days this information relieved me very much. I examined the wound and found it a very bad flesh wound the ball had passed through the fleshey part of his left thy below the hip bone and cut the cheek of the right buttock for 3 inches in length and the debth of the ball. Capt L. informed me the accident happened the day before by one of the men Peter Crusat misstakeig him in the thick bushes to be an Elk. . . . I washed Capt L. wound which has become Sore and Somewhat painfull to him.

—WILLIAM CLARK

After Lewis arrived at the confluence of the rivers, it took him another five days to catch up with Clark, who had continued to drift downstream looking for a campsite free of the clouds of mosquitoes that plagued them. Lewis finally overtook Clark near present-day Williston, North Dakota, where Clark found him lying injured in his pirogue. Here, on August 12, Lewis wrote his last journal entry: "as wrighting in my present situation is extreemly painfull to me I shall desist untill I recover and leave to my frind Capt. C. the continuation of our journal. however I must notice a singular Cherry which is found on the Missouri in the bottom lands . . . some little distance below the white earth river." True to his thoroughness in reporting on the flora and fauna throughout the journey, Lewis went on to describe this "singular Cherry" in careful detail.

Reunited, the expedition continued its return journey, stopping at the Mandan villages to deposit Charbonneau, Sacagawea, and their son. The captains paid Charbonneau $500 for his services, and then sped down the Missouri without any serious incidents with Indians. They were making forty to eighty miles on most days, and eager for the journey's end. Along the banks of the lower Missouri, settlers saluted the expedition from the riverbanks. Popular opinion had it that the Indians had killed the men, or the Spanish imprisoned them.

The Corps reached St. Louis on September 23, 1806, exactly two years and four months after their departure. The ever-diligent Clark wrote steadily in his journal until in St. Louis on September 26, he entered his final comment, which began, "a fine morning we commenced wrighting &c." Of the two, the more eloquent Lewis had not made any entries in his journal for what amounted cumulatively to almost one and a half years, with no explanations given for his repeated silences.